The IT Manager's Handbook

A Guide for IT Professionals and Students

David Miller

First published in 2001

This book is copyright under the Berne Convention. All rights are reserved. Apart form any fair dealing for the purpose of private study, research, criticism or review, as permitted under the Copyright Act, 1956, no part of this publication may be reproduced, stored in a retrieval system, or transmitted, in any form or by any means, electronic, electrical, chemical, mechanical, optical, photocopying, recording or otherwise, without the prior permission of the copyright owner. Enquiries should be sent to the publishers at the undermentioned address:

EMPIRE PUBLICATIONS LTD
1 Newton Street, Manchester M1 1HW

© David Miller 2001

ISBN   1-901-746-151

Typeset by Ashley Shaw and Mike Hubbard
and printed in Great Britain
by MFP Design & Print
Thomas Street
Stretford
Manchester M32 0JT

This book is dedicated to my wife
Judith and to my children
Elizabeth, Sarah and Matthew for
their advice and patience.

CONTENTS

1.	**HANDBOOK INTRODUCTION**	**5**
1.1	Purpose of the Handbook	5
2.	**BUSINESS PLANNING**	**6**
2.1	Business Aims and Objectives	6
2.2	Business Planning	7
2.3	Strategic Activities	10
2.4	Professional Activities	13
2.5	Quality Products and Services	15
2.6	Product and Service Provision	17
2.7	Decentralisation of Services	18
2.8	Outsourcing of Services	19
2.9	Standards and Guidelines	20
3.	**CUSTOMER COMMUNICATION**	**21**
3.1	Customer Care	21
3.2	Communicating with Customers	23
3.3	Telephone and Email Skills	25
3.4	Training Customers	26
3.5	Written Communications	27
3.6	Managing Meetings	30
3.7	Managing Presentations	32
3.8	Marketing Products and Services	34
3.9	Publicity Material	35
3.10	Internet and Intranet Pages	36
3.11	Service Level Agreements	39
3.12	Performance Indicators	41
3.13	Help Desk	44
4.	**PROJECT PLANNING AND MANAGEMENT**	**45**
4.1	Change Planning and Management	46
4.2	Project Management Summary	48
4.3	Project Planning	50
4.4	Risk Assessment	53
4.5	Project Initiation	55
4.6	Project Management Roles	58
4.7	Project Management	60
4.8	Project Status Reporting	63
4.9	Project Budget Monitoring	67
4.10	Post-implementation Review	68
4.11	Quality Assurance	70

5.	**BUSINESS ANALYSIS**	**71**
5.1	Business Analysis	71
5.2	Cost-benefit Analysis	76
5.3	Feasibility Study	78
5.4	Functional Requirements Specification	80
5.5	Proposals to Customers	82
5.6	Estimating Costs	83
5.7	Open Systems Standards	87
5.8	Client-Server Issues	88
5.9	Security Standards	89
5.10	Security in Systems	92
5.11	Data Protection Act	95
6.	**SYSTEM SPECIFICATION AND PRODUCTION**	**98**
6.1	System Specification	98
6.2	Estimating Development Time	99
6.3	Project Timescales	100
6.4	System Design	101
6.5	Database Design	102
6.6	On-line Guidelines	103
6.7	Printed Output Standards	105
6.8	Financial Control Requirements	106
6.9	Process Specifications	107
6.10	Standard Transactions and Programs	108
6.11	Coding Standards	109
6.12	Implementation Planning	110
6.13	User Guide and Training	112
6.14	Maintenance and Support Provision	113
6.15	Work Management	114
7.	**PACKAGES, TENDERS AND CONTRACTS**	**117**
7.1	Package Requirements	117
7.2	Package Proposals	120
7.3	Package Evaluation	126
7.4	Package Benchmarking	128
7.5	Package Risk Management	129
7.6	Tender Questionnaires	131
7.7	Tendering	133
7.8	Contracting	136

Contents

8. STAFF MANAGEMENT **137**
- 8.1 Management Functions 137
- 8.2 Politics in Management 140
- 8.3 Team Management 141
- 8.4 Team Leadership 143
- 8.5 Stress Management 147
- 8.6 Grievance, Disciplinary and Dismissal 150
- 8.7 Staff Development 152
- 8.8 Staff Training 153
- 8.9 Staff Appraisals 154
- 8.10 Managers' Competences 157
- 8.11 Appraisal of Managers 158
- 8.12 Upwards Appraisal 159
- 8.13 Recruitment of Staff 160
- 8.14 Job Seeking 164
- 8.15 Managing Yourself 170
- 8.16 Socialising 177

9. ADMINISTRATION, FINANCE AND PROPERTY **179**
- 9.1 Administration Procedures 179
- 9.2 Health & Safety Regulations 182
- 9.3 Budget Management 184
- 9.4 Property Management 186
- 9.5 Building Alteration Costs 190

10. NATIONAL MANAGEMENT STANDARDS **192**

11. ACCOUNTING TERMS **197**

12. IT TERMS **202**

13. BIBLIOGRAPHY **221**

INDEX **222**

The IT Manager's Handbook

1. HANDBOOK INTRODUCTION

1.1 Purpose of the Handbook

The IT Manager's Handbook provides information technology managers and staff with a comprehensive and practical tool for their everyday activities as suppliers and purchasers of IT services and products. It contains over 300 checklists for carrying out business planning, dealing with customers, planning and managing projects, analysing business requirements, specifying and designing IT systems, evaluating and purchasing IT packages, managing staff, managing one's own career, carrying out administration and health and safety procedures, and managing finance and property. In addition, there are sections outlining the UK's national management standards and defining accounting and IT terms.

The handbook does not replace the need to read around subjects in detail but brings summary guidelines together into one place. It is a document that is easy to read and contains in a concise form much of the detail needed to carry out the daily tasks of IT management. As with any set of checklists, problems should be thought out first and the lists used to pick up missing points. Some of the lists are in a logical sequence for carrying out tasks; others are in alphabetical order.

The handbook will be of assistance to anyone involved with customers, projects and staff, not just those employed in IT and many of the guidelines apply equally to non-IT organisations. The handbook can be used by students to assist with IT and management courses and will be valuable to colleges, businesses and other organisations as a teaching aid resource, to assist with the production of training materials and as a guide for discussion workshops.

The handbook incorporates my 30 years' experience as an IT manager. During this time I observed many occasions when individuals re-invented the wheel when asked to carry out a task. Sometimes this was valid when carrying out new work or reviewing existing methodology but often it was routine work such as recruitment and procedures were already established which should have been used as a basis for further improvement. Occasionally not using tried and tested methods led to disaster when some vital activity was forgotten or an incompatibility emerged. I found it better to document successful methods wherever possible without stifling the need for innovation where appropriate. In addition, written business procedures form an important element of quality service delivery.

In designing the handbook consideration has been given to the UK's National Standards for Operational and Strategic Management and the requirements of NVQ Management levels 3, 4 and 5 including the management of activities, resources, people, information, projects and quality.

Copyright © David Miller 2001

2. BUSINESS PLANNING

All organisations have to develop a survival strategy and draw up a formal business plan setting out their intentions over the next few years. Although the chapter is mainly dealing with the IT organisation itself the issues apply equally to its customers' organisations.

This chapter deals with identifying the aims and objectives of any organisation, reviewing the current business processes and preparing a business plan. Emphasis is also given to running an effective organisation, identifying strategic activities, meeting customers' needs professionally, identifying which products and services to offer, understanding the implications of the decentralisation and the outsourcing of activities, identifying areas where standards and guidelines are needed, and setting out the basis for quality service delivery.

2.1 Business Aims and Objectives

The aims and objectives of an IT organisation are to establish a mutually beneficial relationship with existing and new customers, offering professional quality and cost-effective services to manage projects, to analyse business requirements, develop systems in-house where appropriate, and to assist with the purchase and installation of packages. Customers may be internal or external to the IT organisation.

Objectives of an IT organisation

The aims and objectives of any IT organisation, whether a commercial IT concern in itself or part of a larger establishment, are to:

- Win new customers and retain them
- Form good relationships with customers
- Investigate customers' business requirements
- Propose solutions to customers' needs and estimate costs
- Propose packaged solutions
- Produce interfaces between systems
- Develop applications in-house where appropriate
- Propose and help purchase hardware and software
- Educate and train customers
- Implement systems to fixed timescales and estimates
- Provide support for all types of systems, packaged or in-house
- Obtain value for money in purchases made on behalf of customers
- Set standards and work to them
- Deliver quality services and products
- Carry out effective project management
- Minimise development costs
- Train and develop quality staff to support the IT organisation

2.2 Business Planning

A review of the business, whether the IT organisation itself or that of a customer, is required whenever there is a major change of direction in the organisation and at least annually. This is to ensure that the objectives of the business are still valid and are being addressed and to help minimise the chance of business failure.

Provisionally decide what the key performance indicators are for the organisation and use representatives from each area of expertise to form a small review panel. Use the panel to find out customer needs, to analyse the current and future business against the market place including products and services, their strengths, their markets, the competition, trends in the market and the technical issues.

Review the key performance indicators previously chosen. Identify the technical and managerial skills and knowledge required to carry out the business processes, and the costs and the pricing policy. Decide how corporate culture and policy will influence decisions. Use market research to help forecast the turnover, costs and sales (and cash flow and profit) over a three to five year period. Identify the costs from fixed costs, variable costs such as labour, and overheads.

Decide on the marketing strategy, sales policy, distribution methods, financial accounting, and key success factors for the business and how they will be measured. Identify the capital and staff resources needed, their possible sources and the timescales. Identify the risks involved and how they will be managed. Decide what financial and management information systems will be needed to manage and monitor the organisation.

Draw up a project plan to produce the business plan. Produce a draft business plan that is concise and easy to read, and get an independent check on its viability. Draw up the final business plan with a professional polish and formally present it to prospective sponsors. Implement the business plan, monitor it at regular intervals such as monthly and renew it at least annually.

Business failure causes

Common causes of business failure include:

- An uneven flow of work
- Bad debts
- Failure to persuade potential sponsors to invest
- Lack of experience of managing a business
- Lack of technical knowledge
- Poor cash flow or cash flow forecasts
- Poor financial accounting or management accounting control
- Poor market research or overestimating demand
- Poor quality control leading to a loss of customers
- Reliance on a single major customer
- Underestimating the initial set-up costs and the time to generate a profit

Business review

Carry out a formal review of the business, whether that of the IT organisation or that of a customer, making use of expertise from the appropriate organisation:

- Consider a project definition workshop format for the review (see Project Planning in Chapter 4)
- Consider carrying out a formal business process review
- Involve the organisation's own staff and identify all stakeholders
- Use representatives from key areas to form a panel
- Consider a mission statement and how it will be achieved
- Review the whole of the existing business environment
- Develop a strategy to sustain the organisation through the next five, possibly ten years
- Identify the objectives of the organisation and prioritise them
- Establish the critical success factors for the organisation and how to monitor them
- Identify what the organisation is good at and what the organisation is not so good at
- Find out what customers think, want, and how they perceive the organisation
- Review existing products' quality, price, their life expectancy and customer satisfaction
- Review existing procedures, including IT, capacity, quality, timescales
- Identify new opportunities and threats and decide what can be done better
- Review management information systems and controls
- Review the existing staffing structure, and technical and management skills
- Review work in hand and potential work
- Review existing and forecast costs, prices, income, profit/loss
- Review capital costs and stock, sources of funding
- Investigate rival businesses and their strengths and weaknesses
- Review the current marketing strategy
- Redefine the staff skills and knowledge required to run the organisation successfully
- Decide on the effect of future legislation, green issues, political issues, liabilities
- Identify the risks involved and how they will be managed
- Draw up a project plan to produce a business plan and identify the critical path
- Draw up a draft concise business plan and get an independent check on its viability
- Draw up the final business plan with a professional polish and present it formally to prospective sponsors
- Implement the business plan and the financial and management accounting systems required
- Maintain the plan for changes and monitor actual results against the plan
- Renew it at least annually

Business plan

A business plan is a document required to help examine the merits of proposals to deal with change in a business, to establish practical targets and criteria for the business, and to provide evidence for potential sponsors of the business that the intended direction is financially sound. A business plan for any organisation will contain sections such as those below, which can be adapted to an IT organisation, and will take a three to five year view.

- **Identification:** The organisation name, type of business, address, phone, fax, web site, email address, Managing Director or Chief Officer and the date of the plan
- **Table of contents:** High level contents to give an outline of the plan
- **Executive summary:** Highlights of the plan for those who won't read the detail
- **Introduction:** Reasons for the plan, changes envisaged, potential expansion
- **Business outline:** Products and services summary, short and long term objectives, history of successes, strengths, weaknesses and action being taken, management team, key staff, legal structure, professional advisors; the economic, political, social and technical changes affecting the business
- **Products & services:** Strategy, products and services offered, quality, price, availability, applications, why best, future potential, sources of supply
- **Research:** New areas, improvements, current status, timescales, resources
- **Production:** Development and operational processes, support, problem areas, planning, capacity management, quality control, organisation, premises, tools/stock and their future strategy, key supplies and availability, IT systems employed
- **Customers:** Markets aimed at, customers, size, past and potential growth, market share, customer needs, customer care, competitors' strengths and weaknesses
- **Marketing:** Strategy, customer surveys, methods used, position, pricing, selling, advertising, promotion, support, sales estimates and details, interest shown
- **Selling:** Strategy, current and proposed methods of selling, staff, support
- **Legal & accounting:** Proposals for legal advice and accounting functions
- **Skills required:** Planning, marketing, sales, production, technical, quality, financial, staffing, Health & Safety, IT, administration, legal
- **Management & staff:** Staff for the business functions, numbers, experience, complementary skills, strengths and weaknesses; key staff, responsibilities, abilities to plan and meet targets, motivation; monitoring staff, recruitment, training, cover, use of consultants and sub-contractors, outsourcing
- **Key performance indicators:** Financial controls, sales, production, servicing, marketing, staff, customer care, management information systems used
- **Risks:** The major risks and the intentions to manage them, contingency plans
- **Premises:** Description and location, value, leases, facilities, communications
- **Financial details:** Current and next year quarterly forecasts, following year forecasts, with best and worst estimates for: capital expenditure, profit and loss, cash-flow, return on capital
- **Cost elements:** Rent, leases, rates, water, repairs, fuel, insurance, wages, NI, pensions, training, vehicles, travel, phone, printing & postage, bank charges, depreciation (eg IT)
- **Capital required:** Funds required, reasons, timescales, terms and conditions
- **Project plan:** The project plan to implement the proposals, key decisions, dates, monitoring
- **Appendices:** Such as organisation charts, management team details, key staff details, product technical data, independent reports on products and services, consultants' reports, current orders; previous project estimates, timescales and actual costs and time; recently audited accounts, details of present sponsors and advisors.

2.3 Strategic Activities

Formulate and publish a strategy for the IT organisation to ensure its continuity in times of change. In addition and if appropriate address three areas in terms of an IT strategy for the whole organisation: (i) create and maintain an effective IT organisation, (ii) plan and create an IT strategy for the whole organisation and (iii) assist with the development of departmental IT strategies.

Managing change

Changes in customer demand and IT technology happen so fast that it is difficult to plan too far ahead and it is necessary to create a flexible organisation to deal with and take advantage of change:

- Accept change and turn it into an opportunity
- Create a flexible organisation which can adapt to the changing market and technologies
- Form an organisation structure which is simple with few layers of management and good communications
- Monitor customers' needs continuously
- Offer quality services and products as a first goal
- Allow managers to innovate

Effective organisations

Create an effective IT organisation with the following characteristics and values:

- Be competitive and enterprising
- Be on first name terms across the IT organisation
- Become a leader in the field
- Delegate clear lines of authority and responsibility
- Develop an effective management team that can make fast decisions
- Develop a workforce which is well-motivated, skilled, committed, flexible
- Employ top staff who fit into teams well
- Enable decisions to be made by appropriate managers
- Enable staff to carry out their role with some freedom for innovation
- Encourage effective teamwork throughout the IT organisation
- Have a determination for quality and excellence
- Have a fairly flat staffing structure
- Have a market and customer orientation
- Have a social responsibility (which will also benefit the business)
- Innovate and be optimistic especially to change and turn it into an advantage
- Provide a sound financial basis for operations
- Provide a strong visionary as well as operational leadership
- Provide care, consideration and equal opportunities for staff
- Provide experience, opportunities and challenges for staff
- Put sufficient resources into research and development
- Recognise responsibilities to all stakeholders
- Strive for productivity and performance
- Take a lead in developing a corporate culture and strategy
- Take a systematic approach to change, tasks, problems, decisions
- Take calculated risks and grow the organisation
- Value the workforce and reward performance and quality

Keeping ahead of competitors

To stay ahead of competitors and remain in business:

- Analyse and monitor customer services
- Be outward looking, listen to customers and research customer needs
- Bring in new products at competitive prices and don't rely on a few products
- Concentrate on critical success factors
- Continue to invest in research and development
- Decentralise the main decision making
- Deliver a quality service, the products the customer wants and on time
- Employ good and enthusiastic staff and keep them happy
- Employ supportive financial and management controls
- Encourage good communication between staff and with customers
- Have alternative suppliers
- Keep a spread of customers, not a few big ones
- Keep in tune with the market and competitors
- Keep the market share the business already has
- Provide a rapid and satisfactory response to customer complaints
- Recommend and use modern products which are likely to be stable and have a future
- Retain existing customers
- Strive for customer satisfaction
- Use a fairly flat and flexible management structure
- Use modern production methods

Organisation strategic activities

If the IT organisation is part of a larger organisation, provide input to the whole organisation's published IT strategy and other centralised management activities.

Centralised strategic IT activities include the following:

- Determine the organisation's Information Systems/IT strategy and objectives
- Determine the organisation's requirements in relation to its strategic objectives
- Design and monitor the organisation's IT communications infrastructure
- Ensure the effective use of organisation-wide and departmental IT facilities
- Establish and monitor the organisation's IT procurement arrangements
- Maintain an organisation-wide asset register, especially for IT equipment
- Organise the central purchasing of IT systems, equipment, maintenance contracts
- Oversee the production of annual organisation/departmental IT strategy and plans
- Prepare IT contingency plans for the whole organisation
- Project manage organisation-wide IT projects
- Schedule and monitor the acquisition of IT systems by the centre and departments
- Determine a central policy for user interfaces to IT
- Determine a central policy for data warehousing, maintenance and interrogation
- Determine a central policy for management report production
- Set and monitor 'open systems' standards across the organisation
- Set and monitor professional IT standards across the organisation

Departmental strategic activities

Assist service and operational departments in carrying out their own strategic IT planning:

- Help formulate departmental IT strategy and objectives
- Help define departmental IT requirements in relation to their objectives
- Conduct feasibility studies for IT projects
- Help departments to define and develop projects
- Draft specifications of IT services and systems to be provided
- Assist departments to procure IT applications and equipment
- Prepare IT tenders and advise departments on the selection of suppliers
- Assist departments with the management of departmental IT projects
- Manage the contract with the IT service providers
- Negotiate the best deal for the organisation
- Instigate post-implementation reviews of projects

2.4 Professional Activities

The management and staff of the IT organisation need to deliver a professional quality service the customer will want to buy. In order to do this it will have to act in a business-like way in managing the IT organisation to achieve these goals. It will need to understand and meet customers' requirements, manage the customer relationship, manage the IT organisation effectively, manage projects professionally, and be seen to deliver quality products at agreed prices and timescales.

The customer may be the public, external customers, a part of the larger organisation, another part of the IT organisation, senior management or colleagues.

Managing the IT organisation

Senior management in the IT organisation need to:

- Create a vision for the future of IT in the whole organisation and sell it
- Develop an IT strategy and standards for the whole organisation
- Implement a management information systems architecture for the whole organisation
- Provide direction for IT within the whole organisation
- Establish and maintain credibility for the IT organisation
- Improve customer satisfaction
- Be able to respond to change
- Be efficient, cost effective and performance oriented
- Employ skilled and committed staff who fit into the IT organisation well
- Motivate employees and support them rather than blame colleagues and staff
- Get to know competitors and suppliers in detail and monitor them
- Support the internal business processes through the effective use of IT
- Employ effective work management systems
- Increase technical and managerial skills within the IT organisation
- Demonstrate the success of the IT organisation
- Keep up to date with IT and the whole organisation's future direction

Managing the customer relationship

To provide a professional service the IT organisation needs to:

- Understand customers' requirements and priorities
- Help customers to meet their own commitments
- Advise and inform customers to enable them to make decisions
- Provide services of the agreed quantity, quality, at the agreed price and timescale
- Avoid unpleasant surprises by communicating with customers regularly and properly
- Keep customers informed of the progress of projects and existing services
- Work with customers to solve problems
- Be honest with customers
- Dress in an appropriate business-like way
- Avoid losing customers to other suppliers since it will be very difficult to recover them
- When failures happen work hard to make amends to retain customers

Managing projects

When managing projects for customers:

- Work closely with customers to help them achieve their business requirements and to develop agreement, understanding, respect and confidence
- Participate in the overall planning of the system to ensure a successful project
- Ensure that the customer understands the impact of changes and the need for change control
- Obtain full commitment to the project from all parties
- Use accurate and unambiguous specifications with a formal sign-off procedure
- Use dedicated project management methods
- Negotiate and commit to achievable delivery dates and monitor and control progress
- Communicate and report effectively along agreed channels

Quality service delivery

Lack of a quality service leads to unreliability, extra costs, customer dissatisfaction and customer loss, and to avoid this:

- Continually review the effectiveness of the IT organisation and introduce change gradually
- Encourage employees to review their own jobs and suggest ways to improve them
- Listen to customers' needs
- Deliver systems and services that are fit for their purpose
- Build quality into services and products from the start
- Ensure the reliability and viability of systems
- Give a better service than expected
- Establish a sound service support system
- Establish a disaster recovery plan
- Document business procedures for the IT organisation

2.5 Quality Products and Services

The International Standards Organisation was established as a United Nations Organisation and includes BSI in the UK and ANSI in the USA. ISO9000 lays down internationally accepted standards for meeting quality for any product or service. The European version is EN29000 and the British version (on which the others are based) is BS5750. The standard is a very general one and has been produced to help organisations achieve a 'fit for purpose' standard. All of the standards are similar but ISO9001 is used for one-off products, ISO9002 for standard products and ISO9003 for the development of software.

The DTI will assist with leaflets and advice, as will Business Links (under Business Enterprise Agencies in Yellow Pages). The BSI will advise on a low cost version of ISO9000.

All of the standards are similar and describe the three elements necessary to achieve the standard: (i) put procedures in writing, (ii) train staff to carry out the procedures and (iii) improve the results by keeping records and auditing them. Work to these standards even if not going as far as certification.

ISO9000 elements

The main elements needed to achieve quality standards are:

- Produce an organisation chart and job descriptions
- Document management and staff responsibilities
- Produce written business procedures and make them available to staff
- Control the versions of the procedures in use
- Train staff to carry out the procedures
- Ensure that there is good communication between staff and with customers
- Control the contracting and design processes
- Control the purchase and production of products and services
- Control and record operational production and servicing
- Carry out regular checks and testing of products or services
- In conjunction with the customer identify faulty products and correct them
- Introduce an internal quality audit

ISO9000 advantages

The advantages of adopting quality standards include:

- Procedures are documented and any gaps in them are revealed
- Knowledge of procedures is written down rather than held in people's heads
- Staff understand their roles better
- Staff are less stressed and morale is improved
- New staff are more easily introduced to procedures
- Everyone is involved in quality assurance
- There is reduced wasted effort and hence less cost and more satisfied customers
- Products and services are more consistent in their quality
- The risk for customers is reduced and they have more confidence
- Customers are kept informed of the procedures and can view them
- Some customers may insist on ISO9000 as part of the contract
- The organisation is able to put the qualification for ISO9000 in its publicity

ISO9000 disadvantages

The disadvantages of adopting formal quality standards fully include:

- There are initial costs of setting up the procedures and getting them certified
- There will be on-going costs of quality management (but reduced production costs)
- It may take several years to achieve the standard and cover the initial costs

ISO9000 implementation

When implementing formal quality procedures within an IT organisation:

- Appoint someone to be responsible for quality assurance
- Set up a quality assurance group involving a cross-section of appropriate staff
- Define the responsibilities of the group
- Produce a project plan and get it agreed by management
- Include training and publicity elements
- Produce a mission statement in less than half a page
- Decide on the key factors to ensure quality assurance is achieved and how that will be measured
- Describe and write down the procedures
- Only include the main procedures to avoid an unreadable volume
- Make the procedures available to the staff who need them, perhaps through an intranet
- Ensure that the procedures and documentation are flexible enough for future change
- Implement the procedures, ensuring that staff are empowered to carry them out
- Carry out an internal audit of the procedures
- Register for certification of the procedures if going that far
- Produce a summary of the procedures for distribution to customers
- Publicise the achievement of the procedures
- Get feedback from systems and customers and produce statistics
- Review success or otherwise at management meetings
- Review the processes annually, update the procedures and publicise the changes

2.6 Product and Service Provision

Professional IT services, support and advice are likely to be required in the areas below and the IT organisation must decide which services it will provide, which will be carried out by the customer and which will be bought in from other IT suppliers.

Products and services to offer

Products and services from an IT organisation might include:

- Application development
- Application support
- Business analysis
- Business and technical consultancy
- Changes to existing systems
- Colour laser printing
- Conferencing facilities
- Contract negotiation, completion and monitoring
- Data capture and cleansing
- Data Protection registration assistance
- Data security advice
- Database management using industry-standard products
- Functional requirements specification production
- Geographical Information Systems consultancy
- Hardware and software benchmarking
- Help Desk services
- Input to departmental and organisation-wide systems
- Internet/intranet services
- Local area network installation
- Management reports (assistance with)
- Network services management using network management and monitoring tools
- Network sizing and installation
- Package customisation
- Package evaluation, acquisition, contracting and management
- PC software support
- Post-implementation review
- Printing and mailing services
- Project planning, management and implementation
- Quality assurance and assistance with user acceptance trials
- Software and hardware purchase on behalf of customers
- Stationery design and production
- Support for recommended software and hardware
- System implementation
- Systems integration and interfaces
- Tendering and tender evaluation
- Training
- Unix and PC solutions ('open systems')
- Unix hardware management
- Voice communication services
- Wide area network provision and management

2.7 Decentralisation of Services

The decentralisation of IT functions to users has in many cases resulted from the introduction of PCs and users consequently improving their IT skills, and from a dissatisfaction from users having systems imposed on them by IT organisations. There are, however, functions which can be retained in the centre and the best balance between centralisation and decentralisation needs to be struck.

Centralisation advantages

The advantages of centralising IT services within a larger organisation include:

- A broad or complete overview of the IT operations is more easily obtained
- Administration of IT functions is easier
- Applications, data and systems can be made more secure
- Competition between departments is avoided
- Economies of scale can be achieved
- Standards and priorities are more easily agreed, managed and monitored
- The purchase of non-standard and incompatible equipment is avoided
- There is clear central control of applications purchase and development, and of operations

Decentralisation advantages

The advantages of decentralisation include:

- An ability to react to local needs and monitor departmental activities
- Decisions can be made and implemented quicker
- Departmental staff are more involved in the IT processes
- Innovation is encouraged

2.8 Outsourcing of Services

Outsourcing considerably reduces the IT organisation's costs and enables the organisation to concentrate on obtaining and monitoring the best service from whichever source. This and other advantages have to be balanced against the risks involved.

Outsourcing advantages

The advantages of outsourcing include:

- Bespoke developments are delivered to budget (so long as penalties are incorporated)
- Cost savings are obtained from packages rather than from bespoke solutions
- IT facilities and costs in the organisation can be downsized
- IT management can concentrate on strategic issues
- IT management can focus on requirements definition, purchase and monitoring
- Over-reliance on in-house technical staff is avoided
- PC support and maintenance is cost-effective due to competition
- Professional consultants can help identify solutions to business needs
- Professional standards and expertise are acquired
- Risk management is moved to suppliers who can cope better with risk and change
- Skills can be brought into the IT organisation with few initial costs

Outsourcing risks

The risks of outsourcing include:

- A poor contract may result in problems in the event of a major dispute
- Getting locked into a long-term contract with a product that may become outdated
- More management time is spent dealing with managing contracts, estimates, disputed costs
- Partnership arrangements may turn out to be in favour of the supplier
- PC support and maintenance may be cheap but of poor quality
- Poor outsourcing of software development may leave in-house staff sorting out the problems
- Poor service levels in terms of core systems downtime may result
- Project management may be poor leading to missed dates
- Reverting to in-house services may be difficult once committed to outsourcing
- Staff transferred to the supplier may be forced to sign poorer contracts and may be lost
- Strong negotiation and account management skills are required to protect interests
- Suppliers may insist on using their own methodologies which may reduce flexibility
- Suppliers may be unwilling to deal with the rapid business changes required
- Suppliers may fail to understand business needs and supply inappropriate solutions
- Suppliers may put profits before user business benefits
- Suppliers may recommend expensive, inappropriate or proprietary (non-open) solutions
- Support may involve a number of different agencies and a single contract is essential
- There may be a lack of integration of IT with the organisation's existing infrastructure
- There may be a loss or fragmentation of IT skills within the organisation

2.9 Standards and Guidelines

Without standards nothing would work or get done since human and electronic communication would be impossible. Working to a single set of standards improves human communication, improves system reliability, makes system support and maintenance simpler, and provides a single interface for customers, staff and management.

Create and agree simple and practical but comprehensive standards and guidelines, and make them available to team leaders and their staff in the form of a manual.

Standards areas

Standards areas covered by this handbook include:

- Administration procedures
- Agendas and minutes of meetings
- Audit requirements for systems
- Business analysis
- Business planning
- Changes to systems
- Contracting with suppliers
- Customer care
- Database design
- Documentation production
- Estimating the cost and timescale of projects
- Fault logging and analysis
- Financial controls in systems
- Functional requirements specifications
- Handbook production
- Management reporting procedures
- On-line transactions
- Open systems
- Package evaluation and purchase
- Printed output
- Programming
- Project planning and management
- Quality assurance of systems
- Quality systems production
- Recruitment of staff
- Security of data
- Service level agreements
- Software and documentation version control
- Staff development and appraisal
- Staff management
- Strategic planning
- System specification and design
- Systems investigation and proposals
- Tendering and tender evaluation
- Training of customers
- Work specification and agreement

3. CUSTOMER COMMUNICATION

Getting the correct message over to customers, whether they are external to the organisation or internal contacts, is vital to any thriving IT business. Internal customers include your managers, colleagues and staff.

The issues dealt with in this chapter cover the key benefits of customer care and negotiating skills. They include telephoning, emailing, training customers, producing letters and reports, managing meetings and presentations, marketing services, the benefits of the Internet and an intranet, internal contracting, performance indicators and Help Desk services.

3.1 Customer Care

Nearly three quarters of customer loss is due to indifference to customers and this must be avoided by developing a correct attitude. Build up a good relationship with customers and potential customers to give them confidence that their requirements can be met by cost-effective solutions, that quality goods will be delivered on time and that adequate support will be made available.

Customer care benefits

The benefits of applying customer care include:

- The image of the organisation and customer satisfaction are improved
- Existing customers are retained and new ones gained
- Team working and morale are improved

Customer service attitude

The attitude which needs to be developed in relation to delivering an IT service includes:

- Care about customers and understand their business
- Be committed to providing the services customers expect
- Be prepared to publish the service standards to which the organisation is working
- Understand customers' needs from their point of view
- Care about what actions are taken to provide solutions to needs
- Be confident in answering technical questions
- Know where to get the information from if you don't know the answer yourself
- Learn how to handle difficult or upset customers and staff and remain in control

Customer relationships

When developing relationships with customers:

- Treat all contacts as customers or potential customers
- Envisage how customers perceive the IT organisation
- Each incident is an advertisement
- Look clean and smart
- Smile, including when even on the phone
- Greet people correctly
- Use reasonable eye contact
- Ignore rudeness and insults
- Be helpful and positive about solving problems and don't be negative
- Find out and make a note of those present at meetings
- Understand customers' business requirements
- Ask open questions and don't interrupt customers
- Summarise what has been said at the end of meetings
- Apologise for apparent failures, promise to make enquiries, do so and report back
- Follow up customer complaints promptly by phone and letter

3.2 Communicating with Customers

Develop good communications skills for negotiating with customers, for influencing peers, motivating staff, commanding respect, spurring productivity, when training and when seeking approval for projects and budgets.

Listening skills

Ensure that you are paying full attention to a customer:

- Don't start doing other jobs, listen and don't interrupt, avoid being disturbed
- Sit squarely on to the person and maintain reasonable eye contact without causing intrusion
- Sit forward in the chair, don't fold your arms, look interested, don't make notes initially
- Listen to the voice and watch body language to understand how the customer feels
- Break silences by prompting relevant discussion without dominating
- Occasionally recap and summarise the situation, making notes as necessary
- Understand the problem or requirement and consider possible options
- Discuss possible outcomes of each option and agree on the best option and a standby
- Plan the implementation of the chosen option and jointly implement it

Complaining customers

When dealing with complaints:

- Listen and understand the problem but try to keep it relevant and succinct
- Slow them down – eg by saying 'is this an official complaint?' or 'I'll get a pen and paper'
- For outbursts in meetings keep eye contact until calmer, deal with then or afterwards
- Make use of recapping and paraphrasing and avoid technical jargon
- Make a note of the problem with details of events, problems and the customer's wishes
- Support staff and don't give out personal details
- In letters thank the customer, welcome feedback, reassure of services, ask for clarification, get contact details, propose the next action, sign the letter personally

Negotiating skills

Build up your negotiating skills:

- Ensure that you have the authority to negotiate and make decisions
- Ensure you are negotiating with those who are able to agree a decision
- Build a good relationship with those you need to negotiate with
- Research other participants to understand their needs and issues
- Prioritise the main achievable objectives of the negotiation process
- Prepare an agenda, dealing with general issues first and set a time limit before a break
- Prepare by going over the issues and anticipating problems
- Use arguments which are completely relevant to the cause
- Don't lose your temper and always continue to negotiate
- If necessary tolerate and manage any irrelevance encountered
- Treat non-emotional criticisms as constructive
- Don't be put off by an unwillingness to make a decision
- Don't deliberately expose the weaknesses of the other party
- Keep notes of meetings and telephone conversations
- Both sides need to be prepared to move from their ideal position
- Try to avoid making the opening offer
- Look for opportunities and make concessions that are acceptable to both sides
- Look for ways to allow both sides to feel they have won
- Ensure that you are satisfied with the results before closing the deal
- Consider arranging another meeting if stalemate is being reached and look for fresh ideas
- Consider the use of a mediator acceptable to both parties
- Put final agreements in writing, together with the timescales, and all sign

Persuasion skills

When trying to persuade people to your way of thinking:

- Develop a reasonably firm handshake when meeting people, men and women
- Make a mental note of the person's first name and find a way of remembering them
- Develop a pleasant personality and make people want to work with you
- Develop a pleasant smile
- Address other people's issues as well as your own
- Treat everyone as important
- Give sincere compliments
- Tell people only as much as they can absorb
- Understand the political situation

Bad news communication

When there is bad news to be reported to management, staff or customers:

- Report the problem promptly to avoid rumours on the grapevine
- Don't just deliver bad news but sandwich it between two items of good news
- Use the word 'challenge' rather than 'problem'
- Be tactful, don't exaggerate the problem, don't be negative
- Give the necessary facts having thought it through
- Evaluate and recommend solutions to the problem

3.3 Telephone and Email Skills

Develop a good communication style for the telephone, and treat conversations as though the person were present. Deal with an email almost as if it were the telephone, but remember that it can be a permanent record and may get passed on.

Telephone skills

Look for ways to improve your telephone skills:

- Consider the use of a speaker phone
- Consider using telephone and video conferencing facilities where appropriate
- Be familiar with telephone transfer and other functions
- Know how to respond to answering machines and repeat your name and phone number at the end
- Answer the telephone promptly and within three rings if possible
- Start each telephone call by giving your organisation name and your name
- If you need to transfer a call explain why to the caller and give the extension number
- Alert the person you are transferring the call to and know how to recover a failed transfer
- Note the caller's name, date, time and write down key words on a telephone log
- Use a phone message pad to record calls for other staff
- Use the customer's name in conversation
- If you are in a meeting or need information, promise to ring back at a particular time and do so
- Don't stack up requests to call people back beyond half a day
- Prioritise phone calls and deal with a number of together for efficiency
- Prepare to make a phone call by making notes and questions as a reminder
- Listen, resist the temptation to interrupt, wait for the natural break
- Don't hog the conversation, give the other party time to speak
- Give the conversation your full attention and don't be tempted to do two things at once
- Treat the caller as a valued customer even they are irate, and don't be aggressive or patronising
- Use plain English and don't baffle customers with technical jargon
- Ask open questions and speak slowly and clearly
- Be positive and change 'no' to 'yes, however'
- Sit upright and smile to keep your voice friendly (put a smile in your voice)
- Make notes on the log and read back key points at the end of the conversation
- Finish by summarising what you are going to do and add a final 'thanks' and 'goodbye'

Email skills

Emailing can be a very efficient way of communicating if guidelines are followed:

- Use an address book containing the email addresses of all regular contacts
- Look at email morning and noon and deal with it promptly
- Delete emails you have dealt with, or archive them if they are important
- Take care with the contents of emails since they can be saved, printed, circulated and quoted
- When sending an email check its destination, other copies, subject title, rubbish left in the message
- Avoid unnecessary bulk emails (known as 'spamming')

3.4 Training Customers

Train customers and staff effectively by following basic guidelines:

- Train 'just in time' so that users immediately start using the operational system
- Consider training in two stages: enough to start off with, followed by more advanced later
- Train at the level appropriate to the participants
- Know the subject thoroughly
- Prepare for each session beforehand even when you know the subject well
- Encourage trainees to introduce themselves, their position and their experience
- Get to know the trainees quite quickly
- Be available to the trainees before and after training sessions
- Use visuals as appropriate and whenever effective
- Encourage participation and use participants' experience
- Lecture for short periods with practicals in between to avoid boredom and to consolidate points
- At the end provide handouts backing up the training given verbally

3.5 Written Communications

Set standards for the whole organisation for all written communications including memos, letters, reports, posters, web pages and other publications.

Guidelines for written communications

Use the following general guidelines when communicating written messages:

- Decide what is the main message to be communicated
- Decide on the audience and when to communicate the message
- Decide what is the best way to communicate the message
- Carry out any necessary research to help develop the message
- Involve others in developing the message if appropriate
- Draft the message concisely, clearly, structured, and check it carefully
- Get feedback from colleagues/manager for important messages
- Get feedback on the communication to ensure that the message was understood

Documentation house style

Develop a house style for documents, whether they are memos, letters, reports, posters, web pages or other publications. They should be legible and informative and have a consistent and correct look whoever produces them:

- Keep documents short, interesting, and use concise, simple sentences
- Use short words instead of long ones, avoid foreign words, jargon and abbreviations
- Create a corporate logo: include address, phone, fax, web and email addresses where appropriate
- Use Times New Roman or Garamond at 11/12 point for memos, letters, reports; 10/11 for manuals
- Justify on the left but not on the right unless for a book
- Put the file name/folder left of footer, date in centre, page number on the right, 8 point
- For a manual put the chapter in the header right bold, document name footer left, page centre bold
- Restrict the number of headings to three in a report or a manual
- First heading numbered 'A' etc left aligned bold 14 point capitals
- Second heading numbered '1' etc left aligned bold 11/12 point capitals
- Third heading numbered '1.1' etc left aligned bold 11/12 point lower case
- Restrict the number of headings in a memorandum to the second and third
- For a long letter or memorandum use paragraph headings and page numbers
- Use '•' bullet points followed by lower case for lists; full stop at the end of the last one only
- Avoid inverted commas, over punctuation and capitals; use two spaces after a full stop
- Don't use full stops after 'Mr' etc or after initials
- Develop templates containing the basic house-style elements

Memorandum and letter production

When considering an internal memorandum or letter to communicate particular issues:

- Use memos only as a last resort (it's better to negotiate verbally) or to confirm decisions
- Use the documentation house style (see above)
- Keep memos and letters short and non-technical; if long attach a separate report
- Use a formal format in the first person and draft it at one sitting
- Include contact name, phone number and email address
- Refer to any previous correspondence by date and reference
- Define the purpose of the memo or letter and summarise that in a heading
- List the issues in priority order with evidence, conclusions, actions, closure
- Spell-check and read drafts to eliminate obvious errors, poor structure, poor style, incorrect facts

Report production

Use plain words to produce well-structured reports directed at the reader:

- Use a standard report format for the whole organisation, particularly for the front page
- Use the documentation house style (see above)
- Produce reports that are structured, informative, interesting, succinct and persuasive
- Collect the material and prioritise the issues
- Use diagrams, illustrations, tables and graphs where appropriate
- Draft the report at one sitting then review it with a fresh mind over a couple of days
- Start with a title that summarises the content of the report and date the report
- Include a 'contents' for a long report
- Outline the contents and structure of the report by producing a draft contents page
- Start with the purpose of the report explaining why the report has been written
- Produce an executive summary for a long report (on about half a page) giving the objectives, options, conclusions and recommendations
- Include an introduction giving the background to the report and its logic
- Use headings to enable readers to prepare for the detail and find their way around the report
- Break down the body of the report into sections, each on one subject
- Keep sections short, headed, numbered and broken into short paragraphs
- Number paragraphs (but not excessively) and address one subject using short sentences
- Make use of bullet-pointed lists within paragraphs to give clarity where appropriate
- Add conclusions summarising the options available and the arguments for and against
- Finally include recommendations on the preferred option with timescales, costs and benefits
- Add any numbered appendices (lengthy tables, supporting papers) cross-referenced in the body of the report
- Include a bibliography indicating other relevant reports consulted, their locations and authors
- Add a circulation list to inform readers of the distribution of the report
- Produce the final contents list from the body of the report and have a final check of the structure
- Spell-check and read over drafts several times to eliminate obvious errors, poor structure, poor style, incorrect facts
- Get clearance to issue the report by consulting with your manager and get their endorsement

Document design

When designing general purpose documents such as a poster or a web page:

- Develop a house style (see above)
- Agree a corporate logo, style and image
- Consider other fonts such as **Comic Sans** but don't use more than four font types
- Consider the use of borders, graphics and colour without going over the top
- Start with a title and summary that clearly identify the purpose of the document
- Ensure that the content is organised in a logical and eye-catching way
- Make the document interesting without being cluttered
- Include a contact, address, phone, fax, email and web addresses
- Check for factual, spelling, grammatical errors

3.6 Managing Meetings

When formal meetings are necessary agree the purpose of the meeting, draw up an agenda in consultation with the senior customer and distribute it at least a week before the meeting.

Produce brief minutes (mainly decisions and actions), agree them with the senior customer and distribute them within 24 hours of the meeting.

Meetings organisation

When arranging a meeting:

- Organise the meeting in conjunction with the customer
- Use a meetings planner to book a time when all essential persons are available
- If possible make use of networked electronic diaries to see when people are free
- Only invite relevant people and limit the number of people attending to 12 maximum
- Book a quiet room for the meeting, taking into account travel and the needs of any disabled people
- Meetings are best held on neutral ground in mornings (certainly avoid just after lunch)
- Prepare the agenda and briefing papers with the date, place and time and circulate it beforehand
- Re-circulate the minutes of the previous meeting if necessary
- Prepare for any meeting by reading over the papers and preparing questions
- Keep meetings short (one hour if possible, two maximum)
- Decide whether or not to provide refreshments
- Start on time (no more than five minutes grace)
- Divert any phones to avoid interruptions and get mobiles and pagers turned off
- The chairperson should provide introductions if necessary and not take the minutes
- Rotate the chairperson and minutes secretary for regular internal group meetings
- Organise minutes with actions and timescales, preferably ready to type
- Take apologies
- Agree the objectives of the meeting
- Initiate discussion on agenda items in order, limiting the time on each item
- Ensure that all have a chance to speak by inviting contributions but avoiding domination
- Steer the meeting back to the agenda if the discussion is straying
- Stop cross-talking and secondary discussions
- Summarise decisions on each item for the purposes of the minutes
- At the end of the meeting summarise conclusions and actions to be taken by whom and timescales
- Arrange a further meeting if necessary with date, time, place, purpose
- Thank all for attending and close the meeting

Agenda format

When drawing up the agenda for a meeting don't overload it and produce it on a single side of paper:

- Start with the customer name if there is a customer
- Indicate the purpose of the meeting
- Indicate the date, time, venue of meeting (and how to get there if necessary)
- Apologies for absence
- Minutes from any previous meeting
- Matters arising from the minutes
- Each agenda item prioritised, numbered, time-limited, the person raising the item
- Any other business
- Date, time and venue of next meeting (encourage people to bring diaries)
- Circulation list with organisations/departments, phone numbers and addresses
- Any enclosures for the meeting

Meetings communications

When taking part in a meeting:

- At the start of a meeting be clear about its purpose and the required outcomes
- Encourage all present to participate in the discussion
- Remember that first impressions are important
- Learn how to recognise breaks in speaking and how to signal to speak
- Don't interrupt others and be able to deal with interruptions without being rude
- Be positive and avoid using words like 'can't', 'may', 'try', 'but'
- Agree with others before putting an opposing point
- Persuade through suggestions
- Find ways to handle people who dominate meetings and make inappropriate comments
- Make a few contacts in an unknown audience

Minutes production

When taking minutes for meetings:

- Don't try to chair the meeting as well: instead appoint a secretary
- Take the minutes directly on to a standard form ready to type
- Start with the customer and subject title
- Show the venue of meeting, date, time, author
- List the chairperson and secretary then others present in alphabetical order within organisations/departments
- List those other persons requiring copies including management
- List apologies for absence
- Minute items in the same order as the agenda
- Start each item with a heading and summarise the issues briefly
- Minute the action required on each subject and the date by which action is required
- Include the initials of those persons present who have agreed to action items
- Add the original agenda as an appendix if necessary
- Agree the minutes with the chairperson and distribute them within 24 hours of the meeting

3.7 Managing Presentations

A presentation may be necessary to sell a new idea or a solution to a business requirement. As always, first impressions are important and preparation, style and delivery are key issues in persuading an audience to your way of thinking. Good visuals put a point over better than a lot of words.

Presentation preparation

To prepare for a presentation:

- Book a suitable room, taking into account travel and the needs of disabled people
- Confirm any agenda and travel arrangements in writing, as for the agenda for a meeting
- Organise the reception of the audience if necessary
- Co-ordinate with any other speakers and understand their agenda
- Obtain a PC, graphics projector, overhead projector, screen, flip chart, pens, spares, as necessary
- Prepare the room well beforehand, especially for visual aids and have standbys
- Check over any technical apparatus
- Use a PC presentation package if possible rather than slides or overhead projector
- Ensure power and visual aids work and that you have backups or alternatives
- Check that lighting and window blinds are suitable
- Allow ten times the talk length when estimating preparation time
- Prepare thoroughly, know the subject and make a good delivery
- Be comfortable with the material; rehearse and do a dry run
- Overcome nervousness by rehearsal and practice; using video rehearsals if possible
- Know the audience, numbers, status, background and experience
- Present in a morning and keep it to less than 20 minutes if possible
- Be clear on the objective of the presentation and the main messages to get across
- Structure the presentation in a logical order similar to a report
- Prepare a summary of the presentation with subjects highlighted as prompts; rehearse
- Decide whether to take questions throughout the presentation or only at the end

Presentation management

When actually giving a presentation:

- Make a confident entrance, look smart and relax
- Smile, shoulders back, speak slowly, clearly, loudly to ensure you are heard by all
- Get the attention of the audience and thank them for coming/listening/the opportunity
- Introduce yourself and any supporting staff
- Get the audience's attention and outline the contents of the presentation
- Indicate your intentions about questions and handouts
- Use simple visual aids to illustrate points/keep attention including flip charts and PC packages
- Use a projected bullet list and thus minimise the need to look at notes
- Don't read notes; just pause to check on the next heading and talk informally
- Don't stand too casually, avoid nervous mannerisms and smile
- Look at the whole audience to involve everyone and to get feedback
- Use plain words and short sentences, give practical examples
- Use gestures to stress key points, emphasise important words
- Pause between main points to let the audience absorb them
- Use good humour to get a point over but avoid jokes
- Move around the room or platform without pacing
- Avoid boring the audience and be brief
- Vary the voice and watch for bored signs such as drooping eyes
- Never talk for more than 20 minutes without a break for an interesting diversion
- For long presentations provide interim summaries and the contents of the next part
- Finish on an interesting high note and good humour
- At the end summarise the key points and your main conclusions in one sentence
- Provide references and handouts at the end to avoid distraction during the presentation
- Take any final questions and promise to respond on any you can't answer at once
- If appropriate put forward proposals for further action
- Thank the audience for their attention and any other speakers for their part, and close
- If appropriate follow up with a letter to the customer to stimulate further action

3.8 Marketing Products and Services

In many cases products and services are advertised by word of mouth and through good public relations but it will usually be necessary to carry out some positive marketing of the organisation. Customers may be internal or external to the organisation.

Marketing outline

Identify, anticipate and stimulate customers' needs and identify the strengths of the IT organisation as first steps to satisfying customer needs cost-effectively:

- Draw up a marketing plan with relevant colleagues
- Identify the IT organisation's strengths and weaknesses
- Identify the potential market within existing and new customers through market research
- Identify the competition and its strengths and weaknesses
- Decide on the target areas and identify the customer needs
- Hence decide on the products/services to be marketed and their implementation
- Decide on the price, taking into account costs, competitors' prices and what the customer will pay
- Decide on the way the products/services will be marketed (Internet, newspapers, radio, television, mailing, telephone, sponsorship, newsletter)
- Carry out the promotion process
- Record and monitor costs, sales and cash flow
- Monitor changes in the market and adapt to them (or sales will drop)
- Evaluate the success of the marketing plan

Marketing methods

Choose the combinations of the following marketing methods that are appropriate to the situation:

- Advertising features
- Advertising in newspapers and magazines
- Advertising on public broadcasting
- Articles in journals
- Attending meetings
- Book publication
- Donating products and services
- Free publicity material
- Handbook about the organisation
- Internet and intranet publicity
- Lecturing
- Mailing potential customers
- Networking with contacts
- News and talk shows on public broadcasting
- Newsletter distribution
- Newspaper articles
- Open days, seminars and workshops
- Products/service reviews in publications
- Professional or trade associations
- Public announcements
- Sponsorship
- Standards publication
- Teaching

3.9 Publicity Material

Good printed communications to customers and staff are forms of marketing to make customers aware of the organisation, and to promote its image and services. Publicity can include advertising, a newsletter that can be used to keep customers and staff up-to-date on the business and the latest staff and product changes, and a handbook that can be given to customers and handed out at presentations.

Newsletter

When considering the publication of an IT organisation newsletter:

- Design it to be suitable for customers as well as staff
- Get commitment to regular contributions from all sections of the IT organisation
- Outline the services on offer
- Give an update on organisation-wide projects
- Outline progress on departmental projects unless they are confidential
- Give an update on the organisation's wide area network and Internet activities
- Include software, hardware and network news
- Summarise recent successes
- Outline future plans
- Give management feedback
- Include staff issues
- Encourage contributions to the next issue and give the deadline
- Include the circulation list

Handbook

When considering a handbook for the IT organisation:

- Include the IT organisation's mission statement
- Give a brief history of the IT organisation
- Outline the management structure
- List the business aims of the IT organisation
- List the services offered by the IT organisation (see Product and Service Provision in Chapter 2)
- Reiterate 'open systems' strategy
- Outline the organisation's IT standards
- Emphasise its commitment to customer care
- Describe IT liaison arrangements with customers
- Outline contract arrangements or service level agreements and charges
- Provide a customer feedback sheet

3.10 Internet and Intranet Pages

The Internet and an intranet are inexpensive marketing tools that can be used to reach large audiences and can be used to sell products and services directly. Develop a house style for use on both the Internet and an intranet. Many of the general design guidelines also apply to other forms of marketing.

HTML can be used to set up web pages on the Internet or on an intranet and Java can be used to produce moving graphics. A web authoring package can also be used to generate the HTML but may be inefficient. Information on web standards can be found on the web at www.w3.org.

Internet pages

When designing web pages for the Internet:

- Use a small design team with different skills
- Use communication and marketing experts to do the design but consult with IT staff
- Get the team to visit many sites and develop opinions about design
- If involving an outside contractor ensure that they understand the business thoroughly
- Listen to and understand customers' business requirements
- Decide on the purpose of the web pages and how you will measure their success
- Treat web pages as seriously as any other marketing tool and get management commitment
- Use a short easy-to-remember web address
- Create a house style and a logo, similar to printed documents, and issue a template page
- House style to include the use of colours, graphics, internal and external links, contacts, email
- Minimise welcome pages to enable users to access the information they want rapidly
- Avoid the use of unnecessary graphics on main pages since they slow up page assembly
- Consider designing graphics as optional sub-pages to reduce line traffic
- Avoid the use of plug-ins generally since not all browsers will support them
- Consider avoiding the use of Java/JavaScript since not all browsers/sites support it
- Make use of links to other relevant pages and of the interactive ability of web pages
- Make navigation as easy and fast as possible, including reverting to earlier pages
- Keep the design simple and ensure the pages can be viewed with old hardware and software
- Make an impact, keep the text short and cover generalities rather than giving away secrets
- Offer free useful information and consider giving part of your product free
- Use personal terms in the pages so that customers think you are addressing them directly
- Give customers a contact name to call and an automatic link to email
- Provide for easy printing, feedback and downloading of information
- Draft, spell-check and check the accuracy of statements
- Get someone else to comment on the design, content, taste and impact
- Get management approval of the draft and final designs by short presentations
- Put up a pilot site of the pages to enable them to be seen by the organisation before going live
- Inform management and staff of the web site, and publish its address on all communications
- Ensure that the pages are practical and check them out by using them continually
- Keep live pages up-to-date, monitor their use and feedback and adapt accordingly
- Provide a means of getting feedback from customers
- Monitor the number of 'hits' on critical pages
- Keep a web site under constant review and involve senior management

Intranet pages

Use intranet pages to keep internal customers and staff informed about policy and procedures and to promote services.

The advantages of setting up an intranet include cost and time savings. Staff will be better informed and morale improved. In addition to the benefits of internal email, the whole organisation will be more up-to-date, flexible and paper-efficient. However, resources will be required to manage the intranet, maintain its pages, and enable access. Bear in mind also that the telephone is faster for urgent issues.

Possible subjects for an intranet include:

- Accounts publication
- Data Protection guidelines
- Feedback from customers
- Forms standardisation and distribution
- Handbook distribution
- Health & Safety procedures
- Internal publications
- Minutes of meetings
- Newsgroups
- Newsletters
- Phone numbers
- Policy of the organisation
- Pooling information such as practical tips
- Procedures
- Product updates
- Regulations of the organisation
- Reports to the organisation's senior management
- Services and products
- Staff information
- Training opportunities
- Training practice

HTML basics

The HTML of web pages can be examined by using the View option from the menu. As an introduction to HTML the basics are illustrated below together with some of the named colours. The elements of HTML between brackets are known as tags and are generally in pairs with the second containing '/' indicating 'end'.

- <html> notifies that this is an HTML file
- <head> indicates heading information
- <title>...(the name of the page for display at the top of the browser window)...</title>
- <meta...(text)...> documentation about the code including keys words for use by search engines *
- </head> indicates the end of heading information
- <body> the body of the web page
- <body bgcolor=#ffffff text="black"> indicates body white, text black
- <h1>...(text)...</h1> indicates 24 point heading text
- <h2>...(text)...</h2> indicates 18 point heading text
- <h3>...(text)...</h3> indicates 14 point heading text
- <h4>...(text)...</h4> indicates 12 point heading text
- <h5>...(text)...</h5> indicates 10 point heading text
- <h6>...(text)...</h6> indicates 8 point heading text

- <p>...(text)...</p> indicates new paragraph
- ...(text)... indicates bold text
- <u>...(text)...</u> underlines the text
- <i>...(text)...</i> indicates italic text
-
 indicates line break *
- <hr> indicates horizontal rule *
- <centre>...(text)... </centre> centres text
- <align="left">...(text)...</align> aligns text left
- <tab>...(text)... </tab> tabs text
- <font size= "4">...(text)... </font> sets 14 point
- <font face="Arial"></font> sets Arial font type
- <img src="...(file name)..."alt="...(text)..."> displays a graphics file with alternative text*
- <a href="http://www.(rest of URL)"> (text)... </a> is the form of a link to another web site
- </body> the end of the body of the page
- </html> the end of an HTML file

Those tags marked with an '*' don't need an end tag.

SIZE: 1 = 8 point, 2 = 10 point, 3 = 12 point, 4 = 14 point, 5 = 18 point, 6 = 24 point, 7 = 36 point

If an IMG tag is used as a link to another web site instead of text, it is essential to include an ALT tag after the file name otherwise text-only and speech browsers will be unable to use it.

HTML named colours

Not all browsers support names and the hex value has to be used. However some of the commoner colours are:

Colour	Hexadecimal value
black	#000000
blue	#0000FF
cyan	#00FFFF
gray (not 'grey')	#808080
green	#00FF00
magenta	#FF00FF
maroon	#800000
navy	#000080
olive	#808000
purple	#800080
red	#FF0000
silver	#C0C0C0
teal	#008080
white	#FFFFFF
yellow	#FFFF00

3.11 Service Level Agreements

Service Level Agreements are contracts with internal or external customers for services and are good practice for successful projects or services. They ensure that those involved focus on the delivery of a quality product on time and at the agreed price. However responsibilities need to be clear and the agreement needs to be monitored by both sides on a regular basis.

Service level agreement contents

A service level agreement might contain the following elements:

- The parties involved in the agreement
- Duration of the agreement
- Contacts and signatories
- Standard services to be provided
- Definitions of the services
- Schedule of charges
- Service quality required
- Service availability required
- On-line performance required
- Batch work expected and timings
- Support arrangements
- Security arrangements
- Special requirements
- Anticipated growth
- List of systems and summary of hardware supported
- Arrangements for administration and monitoring of the agreement
- Responsibilities of both parties
- Resolution of problems and arbitration
- Terms and conditions of the agreement
- Charging method and frequency

Responsibilities for service levels

Clarify the relationship between the user and the supplier by defining responsibilities for:

- New project requests
- Minor enhancements to systems
- Change management procedures
- Project planning and management
- Specification production and agreement
- Quality assurance
- User acceptance
- Software maintenance arrangements
- Software support arrangements
- Hardware and network support
- Budget and project status monitoring

Service level agreement monitor

Within a service level agreement, certain performance levels for services or a project will be expected by the customer, which will require monitoring by both sides, such as a comparison of elements of:

- Original ball-park budget estimate
- Agreed original budget from the project plan
- Approved enhanced budget from authorised change requests
- Actual costs
- Original target date for pilot project
- Agreed target date from project plan
- New target date from re-planning
- Actual date of pilot

Service delivery perception

Obtain regular feedback to monitor the perception of services being delivered. This can be built into a service/product sign-off sheet, through independent surveys, or gathered directly from customer and staff contacts.

Keep questionnaires short and simple and use identifiable service elements and measurable scales of service. For example, classify the perceived level of service as 'very good', 'good', 'acceptable', 'poor', 'very poor' (ideally defining what these mean) for some of the service elements below:

- Application support
- Delivery of enhancements to systems
- Delivery of new projects
- Delivery of services on time
- Delivery of services within costs
- Delivery of systems to specification
- Delivery of systems to the required quality and error free
- Documentation quality
- Information about products and services
- Keeping customers informed of progress of issues
- Knowledge of IT
- Management reports and analyses
- Provision of solutions to business needs
- Technical support
- Telephone communications
- Training delivery
- Understanding the customer's business
- Value for money
- Written communications

3.12 Performance Indicators

Service level agreements or business plans will require performance indicators to be devised and monitored for operational and applications services provided by the IT organisation. These are essential to set goals and measure the success of the organisation. Suggested examples of specific and measurable service targets and tasks follow, but it's best to avoid setting too many performance indicators at one time for a particular group of people.

Performance indicators for operational services

Possible performance indicators for operational IT services include:

- On-line availability percentage: average, minimum
- On-line response times such as 80% within 3 seconds, 90% in 4 seconds, 98% in 6 seconds
- Batch work meeting agreed deadlines 99% of the time
- Reruns because of human error less than 3%
- Ad-hoc reports within two hours 90% of the time
- Service failure maximum of one in four weeks
- Maximum downtime per failure of 60 minutes
- Help Desk response times for urgent requests within one hour, minor requests within 24 hours
- Support emergency response within four hours
- General response within 24 hours
- Installation of new equipment within 20 days 99% of the time
- Repairs to equipment within 3 days 80% of the time, 5 days 98% of the time
- Network fault clearance within two hours 90% of the time
- Customer satisfaction levels via regular surveys (maximise)
- Complaints level (minimise)
- Sickness levels (minimise)

Performance indicators for applications staff

Possible performance indicators for applications staff include:

- Administration/management meeting agreed deadlines (maximise)
- Attendance at called meetings (maximise)
- Average time to fix a fault (minimise)
- Clear major faults within 2 hours
- Complaints level (minimise)
- Customer new work budget monitoring accuracy (maximise)
- Customer satisfaction levels via regular surveys (maximise)
- Customer support budget monitoring accuracy (maximise)
- Number of enhancement requests outstanding (minimise)
- Number of reported program faults outstanding (minimise)
- Percentage of overheads (minimise)
- Percentage of time data unclassified (minimise)
- Percentage of time on new work (maximise)
- Percentage of time on system enhancements (minimise)
- Percentage of time on system support (minimise)
- Percentage of time spent on system maintenance (minimise)
- Percentage of unanswered phone calls (minimise)
- Project budget monitoring performance (maximise)
- Project managers failing to meet deadlines (minimise)
- Project profits (maximise)
- Project progress against estimates (through work control)
- Scope work requests within 3 days 90% of the time
- Sickness levels (minimise)
- Staff competence levels (maximise)

Routine tasks for staff

Other possible performance indicators for both applications and operational staff might include:

- Set agendas for meetings to ensure objectives of meetings are clear
- Produce minutes for meetings to a good standard and distribute within 24 hours
- Copy minutes to management
- Liaise with the Help Desk on support issues
- Register change requests to projects and systems
- Scope out the impact of change requests
- Prioritise outstanding work
- Schedule outstanding work and agree new plans within the IT organisation and with the customer
- Negotiate work agreements and monitor and update them
- Supervise project team/resource team to maximise workflow and staff satisfaction
- Ensure plans are available for all main projects
- Hold regular team meetings

Weekly tasks for staff

Routine weekly tasks for all staff could include:

- Meet each member of the resource team to assess progress against targets, discuss issues arising and set targets for the following week
- Review progress on all plans, ensure targets are met and monitor the budget
- Take up any problems with the resource manager/team member
- Update the status of all tasks and estimates of outstanding work

Monthly tasks for staff

Routine monthly tasks for all staff could include:

- Produce monthly progress reports by the last day of the month
- Produce project status reports
- Review progress on appraisal targets
- Record the state of clock cards
- Record sickness this month
- Record leave outstanding

3.13 Help Desk

As part of the service offered, the IT organisation will often set up a Help Desk to deal with all system and hardware queries, faults and orders, if necessary referring detailed calls to support staff. Internal customers may also set up their own Help Desk and the same software should be used to enable calls and their status to be passed between customers and the IT organisation.

Help Desk organisation

When considering setting up an IT Help Desk:

- Understand customers' requirements from a help desk organisation
- Use staff with good communication skills and an aptitude for technical issues
- Organise the help desk hours to match customers' requirements
- Agree priorities on calls with customers and with managers
- Fix as many problems as possible without referring them to support staff
- Aim to spend the agreed amount of time on a call 'on-line'
- Allow some flexibility in on-line time since not all calls will be of the same nature
- Arrange good links with support staff
- Communicate problems fully to support staff
- Monitor progress and escalate issues at the correct time, preferably automatically
- Keep users informed of timescales and progress of problems
- When the problem has been fixed ensure that the user can now use the system
- Meet the customers monthly to monitor service level agreements
- Analyse the reasons for calls and work towards reducing complaints
- Monitor variances in help desk staff and work with them to identify and standardise responses

Complaints analysis

Analyse complaints received by telephone, letter, email or via the help desk over headings such as:

- Software support
- Hardware support
- Network support
- Consultancy services
- Sales
- Billing

4. PROJECT PLANNING AND MANAGEMENT

Project planning and management form important elements for ensuring the success of a project, and these functions are sometimes ignored because of the potential costs, which are often at least 10% of the total project costs. Failure to manage the project properly will lead to failing to meet the objectives, missing the deadlines and running over budget. A large proportion of projects fail to be completed, with half of the problems due to poor communications and the rest due to poor planning and design.

There are several formal project management methodologies in use but many of the principles are similar. The PRINCE methodology is one that is widely quoted and is worthy of consultation. It is important that the methodology encourages taking a pilot right through to the operational stage before committing to other areas.

This chapter deals with change management, project planning and risk assessment. It also covers project initiation, project management roles, managing the active project, reporting back on the status of the project, and monitoring the project budget. Recommendations for holding a post-implementation review and carrying out quality assurance are also included.

4.1 Change Planning and Management

Change planning is about creating the right atmosphere for change within an organisation to enable a project to be successful. Planning will include consulting stakeholders, clarifying user objectives, encouraging users to accept ownership of the project, and the production of a written project plan agreed by all and monitored regularly.

Many projects fail because of the lack of a written specification of requirements, failure to bring users into the project and take ownership, or because of poor project planning and management. The failure rate due to these causes may be about 20%, but in some service areas may be as high as 80%. The scope and objectives of the project must also be clear, together with responsibilities and the quality required.

Change planning

Use the following guidelines for planning changes to an organisation's ways of working:

- Accept that change is a continuous process, partly because of new IT opportunities arising
- Keep up to date with new technology, but be aware of the risks of the organisation leading the way
- Exploit the opportunities that change opens up for long-term gain by the organisation
- Get routine work under control to allow time to deal with more major changes of direction
- Ensure that the change is necessary, justified, cost-effective and improves the quality of the service
- Document the business objectives of the organisation and the change objectives required
- Ensure that the change objectives support the overall business objectives of the organisation
- Ensure that the change objectives are specific, measurable and achievable
- Define the goals required and their relevance to the future state of the organisation
- Analyse the present situation in relation to these goals (where you are now)
- Identify opportunities to produce major benefits for the organisation
- Identify and concentrate on the main essential work processes
- Determine the critical success factors (not too many) and how they will be measured
- Carry out an impact analysis of each change option, document them and decide which option to implement
- Identify the cultural change to the organisation required to achieve the goals
- Obtain a sponsor in the form of the senior manager who wants the change
- Develop the strategies and actions required the manage the change
- Define the changes, the commitments required and the ability to meet the goals
- Get commitment to the change by involving the stakeholders who are affected
- Develop a cultural change programme to persuade those who don't want change
- Present a broad sound plan to senior management to get support
- Agree the objectives of the change with all managers

Change management

Implement detailed changes to an organisation's ways of working along the following lines:

- Hold workshops that promote the values of the changes and get agreement and ownership
- Promote the change as reducing present burdens and bringing new opportunities
- Speak to individuals and set up agents of change in the critical areas
- Provide the conditions in which the objectives can be met, including time
- Involve managers affected by the change in organising the change programme
- Ensure the full collaboration of all resources in the project via the appropriate senior managers
- Assemble project teams with appropriate expertise
- Develop and agree guidelines and standards for the new environment
- Publicise the change through cascaded briefings and bulletins
- Develop educational seminars to be held early on to get the message over and combat fear
- Develop training programmes to be held at the appropriate time ('just-in-time' training)
- Use full project management techniques including a sponsor, project manager, review board, project definition workshop
- Develop a project plan showing the aims, method, activities, roles, resources, timescales, controls
- Identify the risks and include a contingency plan in case of failure of any stage of the main plan
- Organise staff to carry out the change effectively and efficiently
- Implement the change in stages, small scale first, and monitor the results
- Formally evaluate the result of the change, including its planning, to ensure it was effective
- Hold a project end meeting to give feedback and to celebrate and publicise the success

Successful projects

To ensure the success of projects:

- Fully involve stakeholders, users and staff
- Ensure that users, especially senior management, take responsibility for the project
- Ensure that there is a clear vision and that objectives are documented
- Ensure that there is a clear statement of requirements and that they are realistic
- Undertake proper project planning with relatively short project milestones that have deliverables
- Develop a plan that gives the customer early benefits
- Plan so that the project will take no more than about six months
- Plan to take a pilot project through all of the project's activities to test them
- Agree the project plan with all parties and monitor it regularly with the sponsor
- Employ staff with the appropriate skills who are hard-working, focused and fit into the teams

4.2 Project Management Summary

A project will go through a number of identifiable stages from inception to completion as will the plan to manage the project. A project plan is necessary to control a unique set of changes, the outcome of which will be deliverables to the customer. The main elements of the plan will be planning, carrying out the plan, monitoring the plan and controlling it.

Project stages

In outline the stages a project may go through include:

- Make strategic decisions about the project
- Form a project team and initiate project management
- Define and analyse the requirements of the project
- Formally write down the requirements of the project
- Draw up and agree a project plan
- Specify, design and produce or purchase the system
- Contract for the system and for its maintenance and support
- Implement the system
- Hold a post-implementation review
- Provide ongoing support for the system

Project management elements

To control the project, and quite separate from the application requirements, prepare for project management:

- Carry out the initial broad project planning
- Hold a Project Definition Workshop
- Appoint the Project Sponsor, the Project Manager and the Review Board
- Document the project plan processes required in a hierarchical format
- Carry out assumptive planning (assumptions are made about task sizes)
- Produce a hierarchical project plan with milestones and showing deliverables
- Negotiate written work agreements with internal Resource Managers and external suppliers
- Establish formal change management procedures for the project
- Put a project control and reporting mechanism into place

Hierarchical project plan

A method of deriving the elements of a project is to describe the whole project in a short series of boxes, perhaps six to eight. Each box is then broken down into smaller elements, and this is continued until the point is reached where a lowest level box represents an activity to be carried out by a resource manager and their staff. There should be no more than six or so levels:

- Describe the top-level plan in a short series of numbered boxes
- Break each box down to the next level, again using a short series of numbered boxes
- Continue until a series of tasks results that can be carried out by resource managers and staff
- Use the resulting diagrams to build up the computer project plan

Hierarchical plan example

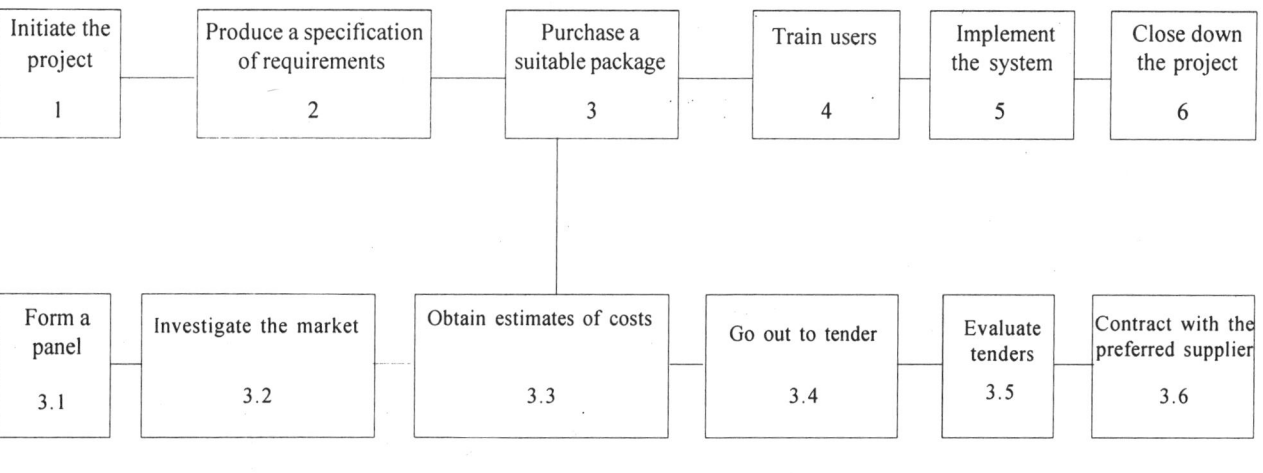

4.3 Project Planning

Project planning is also necessary to estimate the size and type of resources necessary, to establish dependencies between elements of the project, to identify critical paths, to establish the milestones to be achieved and dates together with the deliverables. Planning is also necessary to enable resources to be allocated, to control the project and to enable reporting back to management. Holding a Project Definition Workshop early on in the project involving representatives of all stakeholders will define the project boundaries and encourage ownership.

Project plan attributes

A project plan will contain standard attributes such as:

- Business-oriented milestones with deliverables
- Activities within the milestones
- Measurable tasks within activities
- Types of resources for each task
- Quantity of resource for each task
- Timescale for each task

Project plan example

For example the summary activities for a project plan to obtain a package would be:

- Prepare the business case in conjunction with the customer
- Involve all stakeholders and get commitment from them
- Evaluate the business options
- Prepare a Functional Requirements Specification
- Evaluate the market
- Go out to tender
- Choose a proven system in a reference site of comparable size
- Contract to ensure payment by milestone is achieved
- Project manage implementation of the system with milestones

Project plan activities

More detailed example activities for a project plan are given below. Each of these activities will consist of sub-activities and tasks, with resources allocated against tasks and with target dates.

The activities shown are those milestones which can be monitored at a high level by a project review board, each milestone having a deliverable:

- Agree the objectives of the project with a senior customer to target where they want to get to
- Carry out an initial analysis to establish where they are now and agree it with them
- Form a small group with the customer to model and document existing processes to identify shortcomings and new opportunities
- Produce a redesign of the business processes to give options to meet the customer's needs
- Produce an impact analysis to identify the effect of the changes
- Present findings back to the customer
- Facilitate a project definition workshop
- Produce a functional requirements specification detailing the business requirements
- Agree the functional requirements specification with the customer and other stakeholders
- Estimate the costs of the project from the functional requirements specification
- Carry out a cost-benefit analysis of the project
- Complete an outline project plan with overall target timescales and detailed activities for the first three months (only), drafting the rest of the plan
- Get the functional requirements specification and the outline project plan signed off
- For in-house development produce the system specification and estimate activities' sizes
- Present the system specification to the customer
- Get the system specification signed off by the customer and whoever will operate the system
- For a package produce the invitation to tender and issue it
- Evaluate the tenders and choose a preferred supplier
- Negotiate and sign the contract (to include the functional requirements specification and an outline project plan linked to the payment plan)
- Draw up a detailed project plan for the development/purchase of the software, including data capture and cleansing
- Negotiate suitable resources with resource managers
- Agree the project plan with all stakeholders
- Implement the project plan
- Monitor, control and report progress on the plan
- Carry out quality assurance trials of the system
- Assist the customer to carry out user acceptance trials
- Hand over the system to the customer for pilot running
- Monitor pilot running of the system with the customer
- Hold a formal post-implementation review two to three months after the pilot
- Implement full running and continue to monitor and review
- Provide system support and manage change control

Project file

Allocate and record responsibilities for activities such as sub-project and resource management, budgets, user and IT organisation action and reporting.

The project manager will then maintain an up-to-date project file so that others can take over when necessary:

- Maintain the project file as a ring binder
- List contacts, phone, mobile, fax, email address
- List word processing file references
- File the results of project definition workshops
- File correspondence
- Hold security standards
- Hold organisation standards
- Hold the functional requirements specification
- Detail the budget broken down into manageable elements
- Record costs and comparisons with the budget elements
- File work schedules and work agreements
- Hold contracts
- Keep a copy of project progress reports
- File the steering group minutes
- File the results of post-implementation reviews

4.4 Risk Assessment

As part of the project initiation and planning, identify and assess the levels of general risks and risks in particular activities in the project plan as low, medium or high risk, with 'chance' classified as a high risk. To examine particular risks in activities identify all of the elements of a project, their value to the organisation, threats to them and how the threats can be managed.

General risks

Identify and analyse each area of general risk in the project:

- Ensure that the project has been approved by the customer's management team
- Ensure users have fully defined their requirements, that they are agreed and signed off
- Ensure that there is full support from senior management
- Ensure that there is full commitment to the project from all stakeholders
- Consider whether this project is different from others implemented by the customer
- Decide if this is a new way of life for the IT organisation
- Consider whether users understand the full implications of the project
- Consider any adverse reaction from the trade unions
- Ensure that the system solution is well documented
- Ensure that proven products are being used and have a good future life
- Decide if the project involves unknown product integration
- Ensure that the requirements of performance, reliability, availability are understood and measurable
- Consider whether the project depends on the drive of one person
- Consider whether there are good quality staff available
- Consider whether substantial resources are required for the pilot
- Decide whether delivery dates are realistic
- Ensure that training requirements are understood
- Consider whether an experienced customer project manager is available
- Decide if contracting will be a complex process
- Decide if there any other changes going on which may impact on the project

Risk avoidance

If any of the consequences are high or medium risk, then there is a significant risk element in the project which must be dealt with and that element of the project needs review. Accept low risk but if significant risks have to be accepted prepare contingency plans.

Ways to avoid risks include:

- Provide a proper business case with a cost/benefit analysis
- Involve all stakeholders
- Determine and agree the essential requirements for projects
- Evaluate all options to business requirements
- Produce a formal functional requirements specification and get it signed off
- Use a recognised project management methodology
- Ensure that there are sufficient resources and skills for the project
- Produce a formal project plan, get it signed off and monitor it regularly
- Build quality control into the project
- Carry out independent quality assurance audits

Risk management

Manage the risks through avoidance, passing the risks to others, minimisation of impact and the production of contingency plans:

- Consider the likelihood of occurrence of the risks
- In the first instance avoid risks
- Accept the risk if small
- Transfer the risks to another organisation which can cope (such as a supplier)
- Investigate the impact of risk occurrence
- Produce contingency plans for each significant risk
- Monitor and control the risks
- Carry out a continual review of risks during the life of the project

4.5 Project Initiation

When the broad scope of the project is known hold a project definition workshop to initiate the project formally. The objectives of the workshop include agreeing on the goals and scope of the project, identifying all of the issues and actions required, and ensuring that the people involved in managing the project understand their roles and own the project. Keep the number present to a maximum of ten, representing the various skills required, and record the decisions of the day.

An important feature of the workshop is to get complete agreement from all persons present on all decisions made, such as the mission statement and main objectives. The workshop needs to be led by an experienced facilitator who will organise the meeting, explain the objectives of the workshop, obtain and record agreements and publish the results. The workshop for an average project or sub-project will take a day.

Project Definition Workshop aims

The aims and objects of the project definition workshop are to:

- Initiate the project formally
- Define the project broad boundaries
- Encourage ownership
- Agree a mission statement
- Agree the scope of the project
- Outline current problems
- Agree the goals and objectives of the project
- Identify the potential benefits from the project
- Identify the main risks and how they will be avoided or managed
- Estimate the resources required and the costs involved

Project Definition Workshop agenda

Produce an agenda for the project definition workshop, listing the attendees, along the following lines:

- Introduction by the facilitator
- The scope of the project (broad list of areas to be covered)
- A project mission statement (it is useful to draft one beforehand with the sponsor)
- The goals and objectives (no more than six or seven main objectives)
- The potential benefits of the project
- The changes to the organisation anticipated
- The high-level processes required to achieve the mission statement (a broad project plan)
- The actions and dates required to achieve the objectives
- Major risks, their avoidance and assumptions made
- A broad estimate of costs and resources required
- The immediate actions required from those present with dates for action by
- The management organisation of the project
- Summary and review of the achievements of the workshop
- Closure of the workshop

Project Definition Workshop preparation

When preparing for a project definition workshop:

- Book a suitable room
- Prepare badges for all
- Obtain flip charts (2) and pens, adhesive or drawing pins
- Consider using a PC or an overhead projector for the introduction
- Prepare the ground rules and a draft mission statement from the sponsor on a flip chart
- Organise refreshments and lunch
- Distribute the agenda a week before the workshop

Project Definition Workshop introduction

The subjects to be covered in a project definition workshop introduction by the facilitator include:

- Introduce the participants
- Describe the project definition workshop ground rules
- Emphasise the need for project management
- State the aims of the workshop
- Outline the roles and responsibilities of the sponsor, the project manager and the review board
- Outline the roles of any sub-project managers and the resource managers
- Indicate that the project manager will negotiate work agreements with resource managers
- Identify and acknowledge potential sub-projects
- Indicate the method of recording and publishing decisions made at the workshop

Project Definition Workshop ground rules

During the project definition workshop ensure that all present follow agreed rules including:

- Everyone has to input into the workshop
- The workshop stops if someone leaves the room
- One person speaks at a time
- Participants listen to each other
- All present must agree decisions, otherwise re-debate

4.6 Project Management Roles

As part of the project definition workshop briefing outline the roles of the key managers in the project.

Project Sponsor role

The sponsor will be a senior manager in the main user department affected by the change and whose role will be to:

- Own the project and assume overall responsibility for its success
- Generate the case for the project and gain approval
- Initiate the project definition phase and lead the project definition workshop
- Set objectives for the project manager
- Manage the project manager
- Appoint the project review board and chair meetings
- Agree the project management process
- Agree the project plan
- Support the marketing effort
- Gain backing for project issues and resources at senior level within the organisation

Project Manager role

The project manager will need the usual manager's attributes and in addition must be able to use project management tools, be able to identify risks and manage them and will:

- Be responsible to the sponsor for the successful implementation of the project
- Achieve the objectives of the project
- Maintain the official project file
- Plan, organise and control the work to be carried out via a project plan
- Identify the plan tasks, resources (type and quantity) and timescales
- Negotiate with resource managers for the resources required
- Monitor progress on the plan and address problems
- Report formally on project progress to the sponsor
- Attend and report at project review board meetings
- Organise the marketing of the project

Project Review Board role

The project review board will be chaired by the project sponsor and will consist of a small group of senior managers affected by the change, including the IT organisation, and will:

- Provide knowledge and experience to the sponsor and to the project
- Make decisions on recommendations from the sponsor and project manager
- Review progress against the project plan
- Report progress to senior management in all affected organisations

Resource Manager role

The role of the resource manager is to:

- Manage the delivery of a group of lowest level activities within the project plan
- Agree activities, tasks, resources and timescales with the project manager
- Sign up to a work agreement with the project manager for the delivery of the activities
- Plan and manage the tasks and the staff resources
- Produce the required services to the required timescales

4.7 Project Management

Project management consists of project planning, implementing the project plan, monitoring the progress of the plan, taking corrective action where necessary, managing change, analysing the costs of activities for comparison with estimates and reporting progress.

Project management tips

When drawing up a project plan as the project manager:

- Design the project plan to pilot all activities through to the end
- Plan realistically but don't exaggerate
- Ensure that all tasks are included
- Agree the plan with all of those involved
- Use appropriate and up-to-date project management guides and tools
- Do not take on resource management tasks yourself
- Prepare properly for meetings

Project activities/tasks

For any project of a week or more identify the following elements of a plan:

- The activities required to achieve the plan (groups of tasks)
- The dependency of activities and tasks, that is how they network together
- The tasks for each activity (the effort for a task can be estimated)
- The person to action each task taking into consideration the skills required
- The estimated effort for each task (don't underestimate it)
- The estimated timescales for tasks, hence for activities and for the plan via the critical path
- The major milestones in the plan that need to be monitored
- The deliverables for each activity and milestone

Gantt chart example

The activity and task detail will enable a Gantt chart to be produced with the activities and tasks down the left with their dependencies on each other, person and estimated times for each task, and dates across the top:

Line No	Activity/Task	Depends on line	Person	Estimate on line (days)	Week 1	Week 2	Week 3	Week 4
1	Activity 1	-			XXXXX	XXXXX	XXXXX	XXX
2	Task 1	-	DM	3	XXXXX			
3	Task 2	2	DM	10		XXXXX	XXXXX	
4	Task 3	3	JM	5				XXX
5	Activity 2	1						XX

Project plan progress report contents

On a weekly basis record staff actual time and the percentage completed against each task for comparison with estimates and take action where appropriate. Capture the actual time and the status of tasks from a work management system and produce reports for updates to management.

Produce project plan progress reports on a regular basis (weekly or monthly as required) in the appropriate detail for the project manager, higher management and the customer, mostly extracted from a project management package. Progress reports enable any problems to be spotted and management to be kept informed, including at formal progress meetings with the customer. In addition, extract reports on staff deployment.

Include in project progress reports:

- Customer name
- Project reference
- Project name
- Analysis code
- Project team
- Date of authority for project
- Original approved resources (weeks)
- Extra approved resources
- Used resources
- Percentage complete
- Outstanding effort estimated
- Original implementation date
- Projected implementation date
- Status of project summary

Activity/task monitor

If necessary back up the summary with activity and task details, perhaps as an appendix:

- Activity/task/transaction/program
- Estimated effort (days)
- Used effort
- Percentage complete
- Outstanding effort

Project status review

Organise a more formal review of the status of the project with the review board at a suitable checkpoint perhaps once a month:, reporting on progress against the plan and goals for the next monitoring period:

- Report on the status of milestones and deliverables
- Report on the project timescale achievements
- Report on the use of project resources
- Give feedback on budget monitoring
- Report on progress towards meeting the project objectives
- Indicate any deviations from the plan and actions being taken to correct these
- Give management support status
- Report on the status of support provided by the user
- Propose the next checkpoint for approval by the board
- Indicate the next milestones to be monitored

Project plan bad news

If there is bad news to report back to the review board, consult with the sponsor:

- State the news and don't obscure it, but also report good news first
- Report the bad news promptly to avoid the grapevine
- Provide the relevant history and facts
- Re-plan the project since the original assumptions will no longer be valid
- Suggest alternative courses of action with the pros and cons of each
- Look for any positive opportunities that can be taken
- Provide recommendations and how they will address the problem
- Provide a new plan and goals for approval
- Summarise the key points

4.8 Project Status Reporting

When reporting back to the project review board produce a formal and detailed project status report, to supplement a project plan presentation, containing the following sections:

Project identification

Identify the project:

- Customer name
- System name and identity
- Project name and reference
- Date project initiated
- Pilot system target date
- Cost code (such as customer/system/contract)

Project managers

Identify the managers of the project:

- Sponsor and phone number
- Project manager and phone number
- IT business analyst and phone number

Project summary

Summarise the reasons for the project and its requirements:

- The reasons for the change with benefits and cost savings
- The business requirements summary

Project approval dates

List the dates the main stages of the project received approval such as:

- Approval for the project by the customer
- IT organisation approval
- Resources identified and approved
- Investigation of requirements
- Functional requirements specification
- Scoping (estimating the impact)
- System specification
- Project plan
- Resource allocation
- Development/acquisition of system

Change approval

Document approval of any recent changes to the scope of the project, showing for each:

- Date of the latest change requests to the IT organisation
- Date of latest costings from the IT organisation
- Date authority given to the IT organisation for the changes
- Date the IT organisation resources were scheduled
- Estimated completion date
- Cost code (such as customer/system/contract/change)

Project resources summary

Summarise the total use of IT organisation and customer resources:

- IT organisation weeks estimated from the system specification
- Enhanced weeks from approved changes
- Contract price
- Training weeks estimate
- Customer weeks estimate
- Total capital cost

Project status report

Summarise the target date and costs to date:

- Today's date
- Pilot target date from the original plan
- Latest target date from re-planning
- Actual date of pilot
- Latest weeks estimated from re-planning
- Weeks used to date
- Costs to date
- Percentage completed
- Estimated weeks outstanding
- Projected cost of the project

Milestones progress report

Report on the status of key milestones and deliverables such as:

- Project definition workshop results
- Cost-benefit analysis completion
- Outline project plan approval
- The detailed project plan completion
- Contracting/service level agreement
- Resource scheduling and work agreements
- Functional requirements specification completion
- System specification (required for in-house development)
- Package evaluation and recommendation
- The tendering process and the selection of a preferred supplier
- Approval of the preferred supplier by the customer's management
- Acquisition/development of the system
- Hardware and software installation and commissioning
- User acceptance trials
- User training
- Pilot/parallel running
- Full operational running
- Post-implementation review (after the pilot and/or after full running)

Change summary report

Report on the progress of project changes (and faults) during a major project and present a summary of changes to the customer and IT management:

- System/project name and code
- Change/fault reference number
- Description of the change/fault
- Date the change/fault was notified
- Source of the request
- Priority rating (high, medium, low)
- Authority for implementation
- Agreed delivery date
- Status of the change
- Date accepted by the user

Projects' status summary

Report the progress of all projects to customers and IT management in summary form for each project for each customer:

- Customer and project name
- IT organisation project manager
- Resources (if used as an IT organisation document)
- Project plan production status
- Original target date agreed with the customer
- Current stage reached
- Next stage planned
- Project implementation target and details
- Budget reference and cost code
- Original budget for the contract
- Additional budget agreed through contract variations
- Costs to date and projected costs

4.9 Project Budget Monitoring

Monitor the various budgets agreed with the customer for each project, for all new projects, and for support and maintenance of existing systems.

To enable this to take place activities need classifying as non-chargeable (such as scoping), support and maintenance, or new work, and monitored against their budgets for each customer, system and project. Consider charging support and maintenance at 15% of a system's current value and ensuring that the non-chargeable scoping/feasibility costs are less than 2½% of the value of the scheme.

Project budget monitor

Produce regular (such as weekly) reviews of costs against budgets for each project whether or not presenting them to the customer or IT management and use them to monitor the financial status of the project:

- Customer and project name
- Monitoring period end date
- Original agreed target date
- Budget price
- Enhanced budget following approved changes
- Costs to date
- Percentage completed
- Days/weeks outstanding
- New target date
- Targets to be completed for next monitoring period

4.10 Post-implementation Review

About three months after the implementation of a project, review its success and lessons to be learned by investigation and interviews followed by a formal meeting to present and discuss the results with the customer and IT management. Put the results in writing and use them to report to senior management and for future reference. If the customer is satisfied that the system meets the original specification get it signed it off.

Post-implementation review terms of reference

Agree the terms of reference of the post-implementation review with the senior customer, such as:

- Review the success of the project management process
- Review the selection and acquisition process
- Identify the goals and key objectives of the project
- Review whether the goals and the objectives were correct
- Determine whether the goals and objectives have been met
- Measure the benefits and savings against those predicted
- View the main functionality of the system
- Interview management and users re fitness for purpose of the system
- Review suppliers' successes and failures
- Review relationships between all parties
- Check the efficiency of the system
- Review the IT costs against the budget
- Identify and document successes and problems, and get feedback for the future
- Document conclusions and recommendations
- Discuss the draft report with IT management
- Present the draft report to the customer
- Present the final report to the project review board
- Continue to review the system annually

Post-implementation review report

Following interviews and fact-gathering prepare a short summary report to present to the project review board:

- Project name and short description
- Identify the original objectives and the benefits of the change
- Discuss whether the objectives and benefits were met
- Identify any operational problems encountered
- Report any project management problems
- Outline successes and failures
- Review actual costs against estimates
- Propose changes to good practice

Project resource analysis

For the benefit of the IT organisation at the end of the project and as part of the post-implementation review analyse staff resources by activity and review income against costs. Compare with both the original and final estimates to improve the estimating of future projects. Block any further booking of time to the project.

Compare costs and income for:

- Scoping and feasibility
- Business consultancy and functional specification production
- System specification, design and prototyping
- Program specification
- System coding and testing
- Systems trials and user acceptance trials
- Package acquisition including tendering and contracting
- Package tailoring and links to other systems
- Implementation of the system
- Training of customers
- Project management
- Post-implementation support
- Minor enhancements
- Fault correction

Project profit monitor

Again, solely for the IT organisation's information, when the project has been completed and signed off by the customer at a post-implementation review:

- Take the initial firm estimate for the project, authorised by the user
- Add charges for authorised changes
- Subtract new work costs
- Subtract support costs for the project before handing over fully live
- The net figure is the profit on new work, which should be targeted at 5% to 10% or some other agreed figure

Support and maintenance profit monitor

Similarly, to monitor the support and maintenance profit situation on any particular system or service at the end of a budget period:

- Take the support and maintenance budget from the service level agreement or contract
- Subtract system support and maintenance actual costs
- The net figure is support profit

4.11 Quality Assurance

Provide quality assurance of IT systems to meet customers' expectations by building quality throughout the service or product and continually monitoring it, without expending extra cost or time if possible. Follow the ISO9000 guidelines described earlier even if not intending to register for certification.

Quality assurance practicalities

To achieve a quality service or product:

- Involve the staff in developing a quality service plan to get their commitment
- Document management and staff responsibilities
- Provide the right quality of staff to deal with customers
- Set up good internal communications
- Liaise with all customers to understand their needs
- Develop a good specification of customer requirements
- Design a comprehensive system as if you were a user
- Set and monitor good standards including security
- Use standard application package selection procedures and criteria
- Use standard programming designs for in-house work
- Provide and maintain the correct level of good quality documentation
- Carry out thorough project planning, project management and change control
- Monitor the production/acquisition process against the specification of requirements
- Link the payment profile in the contract to major milestones completion
- Sign off milestones in the project with the customer
- Carry out on-line and batch systems trials for in-house systems
- Carry out formal independent systems trials using standard test data for in-house systems
- Advise the customer in carrying out user acceptance trials
- Run in parallel with any existing batch system if possible, reconciling any differences
- Introduce the system as a pilot of a small area, either geographically or functionally
- Monitor the pilot and final operational systems
- Arrange rapid but thorough corrective action if problems occur
- Carry out internal audits of quality including standards and security
- Obtain feedback from customers on their perception of IT services and products
- Provide feedback to staff on their performance
- Hold a post-implementation review of successes and failures with the customer

5. BUSINESS ANALYSIS

Business analysis is the process of reviewing an organisation's objectives and how it achieves them, with a view to improving efficiency and effectiveness. The analysis will be carried out by consulting its stakeholders in a review with a senior customer and through finding out what is done, how, why, when and where.

This chapter deals with the process of business analysis, cost-benefit analysis, feasibility study, the production of a functional requirements specification and presenting proposals to customers. The methods of scoping projects and estimating costs are given, together with the advantages of employing open system standards and the issues involved when considering client-server systems. Data and system security standards are explored and the Data Protection Act is summarised.

5.1 Business Analysis

Procedures within the business can be thought of as systems with life cycles whereby changed business needs lead to the need to establish new objectives and hence start the cycle again.

System life cycle

From the IT organisation's perspective a system or project may go through the following stages:

- Receive a request for help because of new organisation policy, legislation or technology
- Establish the objectives of the system and prioritise them
- Carry out a feasibility study of the proposed changes
- Produce a project plan and agree it with a steering group
- Analyse and define the new requirements in more depth
- Produce a functional requirements specification
- Purchase the system (or design, build and test) and install it
- Carry out user acceptance testing
- Plan and execute the implementation of pilot and live systems
- Monitor the pilot and live systems
- Review and evaluate the system and the plan
- Support and maintain the system and keep it updated

Business process review

Review the whole of the business processes or just a system as required.

Identify the stakeholders, interview stakeholder representatives, understand the structure of the business and its objectives, document the present procedures and their costs and performance, and identify new requirements:

- Carry out the business process review early in the project
- Describe the business analysis methodology to the senior customer
- Agree the objectives and scope of the project with the senior customer
- Get authority to carry out the work and agree its terms of reference
- Find a user partner or set up a small team to make best use of expertise
- Obtain and review statements of company or organisational policy and objectives
- Identify the aims and objectives of the organisation and prioritise them
- Identify the key performance criteria of the business and how they are measured
- Understand the structure of the customer's organisation and stakeholders
- Identify and consult representatives of all stakeholders
- Encourage the senior customers to describe their particular needs
- Use work flow diagrams and data models to map current data structures and flow
- Completely review the objectives and the current processes to achieve them
- Identify better ways to achieve the aims and objectives of the business
- Look at quality control procedures and identify areas for improvement
- Follow the ISO9000 guidelines on quality

Stakeholder identification

Stakeholders of a system may include:

- Customers
- Employees of the organisation
- Users of the system
- The public
- Suppliers of goods and services
- Other organisations
- Management

Stakeholder interviews

When carrying out interviews of stakeholders:

- Identify the best representatives of the stakeholders
- Make appointments to see them and give the reason
- Carry out background reading of the organisation
- Prepare prompting questions and consider a standard form
- Encourage the interviewee to talk by asking open questions
- Record the information in summary form (warn the interviewee)
- Check the information for accuracy against details already gleaned
- Type up the summary and copy it to the interviewee

Business structure identification

Investigate the structure and basic procedures of the organisation and agree it with a senior customer:

- Document the organisation structure and locations
- Obtain statements of organisation policy and objectives
- Document the service production arrangements
- Document purchase and supply arrangements
- Document financial accounting arrangements
- Document management accounting arrangements
- Outline the sales, marketing, research, personnel and administration organisations
- Document the hardware, networking and software strategy

Current systems appraisal

Investigate the customer's current systems with a partner from the organisation:

- Set up a small project team with the customer
- Obtain statements of business policy and business objectives
- Determine to what extent the objectives are met
- Document details of business procedures
- Obtain specimens of documents in use
- Determine current data structures, data responsibilities and data flow
- Document interfaces with other systems, internal and external
- Detail volumes of records and transactions
- Document timings of batch and on-line processes
- Compare findings with the hardware, networking and software strategy
- Identify legal and organisation policy constraints
- Document the present costs of the system
- Agree the findings with the partner or team

Functions identification

Identify and list the current main business functions of the organisation:

- Description each business function
- Detail volumes
- Identify the service levels required
- Document the input/output processes
- Identify data access requirements
- Describe the processing for each function
- Document the timings required

System performance appraisal

Investigate and document how well the present system works:

- Identify the costs of the present system
- Document on-line response times and availability
- Document the batch timings
- Investigate the accuracy and quality of the system
- Analyse the reliability, security, capacity of the system
- Investigate the flexibility, efficiency, acceptability of the system
- Document any key performance indicators and how well they are met

Costs appraisal

Document the current costs of the system for:

- Staffing
- Materials
- Equipment
- Operating expenses
- Leases on capital
- Overheads

Business requirements

Through interviews identify the perceived new requirements, scope them out, document them and agree a preferred solution:

- Identify problems and new requirements from users and management
- Consult representatives of all stakeholders and unions
- Challenge existing long-standing procedures
- Define and prioritise the new objectives and any constraints
- List the issues, effects, volumes, links to other systems
- Identify the source, the owner, and the priority of issues
- Define security, control and audit requirements
- Suggest potential solutions, benefits, impacts, costs
- List the main functions required, volumes, timings
- Produce draft business options, benefits and budget costs
- Agree the preferred option with the project team
- Produce/assemble a prototype system and demonstrate it to users
- Estimate the final costs
- Report the findings and present them to management for agreement

System review

Sometimes a quick review of a system and its processes can be very productive in immediately identifying shortcoming and improvements using a 'think-tank' with a few stakeholders:

- With a senior customer or two and an IT partner review any previous analysis
- Use a label for each process summarising input, processing, output, links
- Stick the labels on the wall ready for discussion and review with the group
- Go over each stage and identify shortcomings and opportunities
- Note the shortcomings and opportunities in two further colours on the labels
- Agree on and document the way forward
- Organise a presentation to senior management in the user organisation to get support

5.2 Cost-benefit Analysis

A cost-benefit analysis can be used to help make a decision on a proposal, and consists of identifying the benefits (such as increased income, reduced costs or improved services), the costs and the pay-back period. The pay-back period must be short such as one or two years, and there must be evidence to support this. It can also identify the costs and benefits of existing arrangements.

Tangible benefits can be measured more easily than the intangible ones, although all benefits can be estimated.

Project cost areas

Project cost areas may include:

- Additional staff and salary increases
- Applications
- Communications, cabling, routers, switches, lines
- Compliance with European and Health & Safety regulations
- Consumables
- Data collection, validation and cleansing (correction and modification)
- Data conversion
- Data identification
- Data maintenance
- Data preparation and capture
- Delivery and installation of hardware and software
- Furniture
- Hardware purchase
- Network points and power
- Operational and technical training
- Overheads such as building and security
- Packages
- Project management
- Requirements analysis
- Software customisation
- Software development
- Software evaluation
- Software installation
- Software licences
- Software purchase
- Specialist support
- Standards compliance
- Systems interfaces
- Systems software
- Transitional costs

Tangible benefits

Possible tangible benefits of a change might include:

- Accommodation savings
- Avoidance of costs
- Greater speed of production
- Improved asset management
- Increased income opportunities
- Lower costs of data archiving and retrieval
- Lower costs of data management
- Lower costs through automation
- Materials savings
- Productivity improvements
- Reduced capital expenditure
- Reduced effort to produce management information
- Staff savings

Intangible benefits

Intangible benefits of a change might include:

- Ability to deploy existing resources more accurately
- Ability to integrate sets of data and provide better access to information
- Ability to monitor policy implementation and performance measures
- Ability to undertake more rigorous data management
- Better cash flow
- Better management information
- Compliance with statutory needs
- Fulfilment of service objectives
- Greater reliability
- Improved ability to bid for additional resources
- Improved ability to meet requirements of new regulations and new legislation
- Improved access to shared data through the adoption of standards
- Improved communications
- Improved customer satisfaction
- Improved data security
- Improved quality of information
- Improved services to customers (internal and external)
- Improved staff satisfaction and opportunities
- Opportunities for management by exception
- Opportunities to cleanse existing records as part of the data capture process
- Reduced downtime
- Reduced potential for administration failure and legal liability

5.3 Feasibility Study

For larger projects, a feasibility study will be required whether or not a formal method of systems analysis and design such as SSADM is to be used in investigating and designing the system. This will give a broad estimate of the cost and enable the full project to be considered for authorisation. A feasibility study differs from business analysis in scale and is aimed at a specific project rather than a review of the whole business processes.

Establish broad terms of reference and agree them with all management bodies to define the scope of the project before the study is started. Undertake investigation to establish details of the current and required systems and record and file the findings.

Following the feasibility study, obtain agreement to go ahead by means of a formal report to management or steering group. If reporting to a senior management group rather than a project steering group, summarise the information in the form indicated in the 'report production' section.

Feasibility report

The contents of a feasibility study report might include:

- Customer, organisation and date of the study
- Project name and summary
- Person carrying out the study
- Report contents list
- Purpose and scope of the study
- Terms of reference such as objectives, scope, constraints, timescales and resources
- Executive summary on half a page
- Introduction and background
- Customer's management structure
- Departments, sections and managers
- Business objectives prioritised
- Key performance indicators and how they are monitored
- Broad business procedures involved
- Broad data flow
- Input and output of the main procedures
- Data frequencies, origins, destinations, volumes and timings
- Interfaces to other sections and systems
- Security and audit arrangements
- Financial and management accounting issues
- Other support services involved
- Quality control arrangements
- On-line functions and the availability of systems
- Reporting and batch functions and their timings
- Relationships between departments, sections, outside bodies
- Costs of the present system and the method of charging
- Shortcomings of the present system and new business requirements
- Possible business solutions, advantages and disadvantages
- Cost-benefits and service-benefits of the solutions
- Staffing implications
- The preferred business solution
- Possible phases of a new system
- Staffing and training implications
- Data Protection, security, audit and control requirements
- Success factors and their measurement
- Broad implementation plan and timescales
- Application, hardware and network likely costs
- IT organisation and customer resources
- Capital and running costs and resources, five year costs
- Further development areas for the future
- Conclusions and recommendations
- Bibliography
- Appendices

5.4 Functional Requirements Specification

Whether or not a full analysis of requirements has been carried out as above, produce a functional requirements specification to record the business requirements of the new system formally.

Note any decisions on system requirements agreed by the project steering group as a list until requirements begin to stabilise. Having investigated and agreed on the broad solution to the customer's requirements add further detail as the requirements are firmed up to become the functional requirements specification.

Develop the functional requirements specification as four main sections plus any appendices: (i) the identification of the system, (ii) the business requirements as perceived by the customer, (iii) the detailed application requirements as jointly agreed by the customer and the IT analyst, and (iv) the application and operational technical requirements as specified and collected by the IT organisation.

Expand the functional requirements specification to become the full systems specification for an in-house development (see System Specification in Chapter 6).

System identification

Identify the system for which a functional requirements specification has been produced:

- Organisation name
- Project title
- Customer
- Sponsor of the project
- Author of the specification and date
- Signed off by and date
- Table of contents

Business requirements

Encourage the customer to take a lead in producing the business requirements section in the format:

- Introduction
- Purpose of the document
- Organisation summary
- IT strategy in terms of hardware, networking and software
- Customer organisation and objectives
- IT organisation and objectives
- Summary of business requirements
- Policies and constraints
- Key objectives to be met and their benefits
- Main functions to be carried out
- Future requirements
- Timescales envisaged and possible phases
- Outline project organisation and plan

Application requirements

Produce the application requirements jointly with the customer, detailing the functionality required by all users:

- Data and user volumes
- System access and security
- Administration and housekeeping
- Audit trail requirements
- Financial controls and statistics
- Function specification (a list of the business transactions required)
- Main data flow and procedures
- Interfaces to other internal systems and to external systems
- Analyses and reports
- Ad-hoc reports
- Batch functions
- Financial and procedural controls
- Help system
- Standing data outline
- Data capture and cleansing outline
- Archiving requirements
- Data Protection requirements including data retention
- Performance requirements
- System availability and resilience levels required
- Possible future phases

Technical requirements

If going out to tender add the technical requirements section:

- IT standards for the organisation including open systems
- System environment
- System conventions
- Hardware requirements
- Network requirements
- Operational requirements
- List of transactions envisaged
- Volumes of main types of data and transaction rates
- Print volumes and deadlines
- On-line users: concurrent and maximum
- Project management guidelines
- Draft project plan

Functional Requirements Specification appendices

Add any appendices to the functional requirements specification such as:

- Reference to any preceding feasibility work
- Cross-references to backing documentation
- Organisation standards such as security, open systems

5.5 Proposals to Customers

Following the investigation of a scheme, the IT organisation is in a position to bid for the work, and this can be in the form of the functional requirements specification to which the services and intentions of the IT organisation have been added and called a System Proposal.

Use the document to sell the proposed solution to the customer's business requirements, professionally package it and present it to the customer formally.

Get the system proposal signed off by the customer in stages to enable early phases to be implemented while the later ones are being developed.

As part of the formulation of a system proposal, it may be possible to prototype the transactions with the customer to enable the formal agreement on the required system to be reached more rapidly. Prototyping assumes that some form of screen/print manager or Fourth Generation Language is available, which will allow rapid changes to formats to be made and viewed. Impose strict limits on the number of prototype versions produced, perhaps three, or on the total time to be spent on prototyping, or it will never end!

System proposal contents

Base proposals on the functional requirements specification and add:

- A table of contents
- Purpose and scope of the proposal
- Approach to the business need to meet the terms of reference
- The benefits of the approach
- The development envisaged
- The development environment
- Design considerations taken into account
- Development timescales
- The phases envisaged
- Conventions and standards proposed including security and audit
- Project management arrangements and responsibilities
- Progress reports and milestone monitoring
- Initial set up costs and running costs
- Personnel requirements from the supplier and the customer
- Senior management support and steering body arrangements
- Customer service level agreement arrangements

5.6 Estimating Costs

Whether for the purposes of giving a quick assessment of a new IT scheme or for giving an estimate of the cost of a change to an existing system, use a standard form for change control and scoping (see Work Management in Chapter 6), and estimate the various resources required. Don't underestimate costs since running over will give the IT organisation a bad reputation. Unit costs will vary according to installation and over time and actual rates are not given below.

Derive staff costs and hence charges from salary plus overheads. To enable senior staff to produce estimates for customers publish schedules of services and hardware rates also. Review the rates regularly and republish.

Staff charging rates

To arrive at a daily charging rate for an employee:

- Start with the annual salary (or the average for a group of employees)
- Add 20% for National Insurance and pension contributions
- Add overheads from management, finance and administration (add 100% if not known)
- Add any percentage profit aimed at, perhaps 5% to 10%
- Divide by the number of working days in the year (say 200)

Staffing estimates/recharges

It will probably be necessary to divide staff up for recharge rates according to the type of work they do such as:

Staffing estimates	Rate	Annual cost
Consultancy	£/day	
Development	£/day	
System support	£/year	15% of system value
Network staff	£/day	
Technical support	£/day	
Operational support	£/day	

Operations estimates

It will probably be necessary to divide operational services up for recharge rates according to the type of work such as:

Operations estimates	Rate	Annual cost
Mainframe time	£/unit	
On-line transactions		£/workstation/year
Batch programs	£/hour	
Line printing	£/hour	
Laser printing	p/side	
Mailing (excluding postage)	p/letter	
Mail inserts	p/insert	
Pressure sealing	p/letter	
Microfiche original	p/fiche	
Microfiche copy	p/fiche	

Network costs

Publish schedules of standard network hardware items such as:

Network item	Rate	Annual cost
Power socket	£	
Structured cabling	£/dual socket	
Kilostream line (cost depends on distance and speed)	£	£
ISDN line	£	£ plus calls
Router	£	£

Workstation costs

Publish schedules of standard workstation items such as:

Workstation item	Capital cost	Annual cost
File server including network licence	£	£
Structured cabling per dual socket	£	
PC + LAN card + software	£	£
PC alone	£	£
Network (LAN) card	£	
Laser printer	£	£
Colour printer	£	£
Internal fax-modem	£	
External modem	£	
Software costs	£	

Publish schedules of standard software such as:

Software	Capital cost	Annual cost
Microsoft Office		£
Lotus Smartsuite		£

Unix costs

Publish schedules of standard Unix items such as:

Unix item	Capital cost	Annual cost
Disk space	£/gigabyte	
Relational database run time licence	£ £/seat	
Management reporting package	£/seat	

Telephone costs

Publish schedules of standard telephone equipment such as:

Telephone costs	Capital cost	Annual cost
Telephone	£	£
Extension	£	£
Feature phone	£	£

Hardware requirements

Assess any effect on existing centralised processors and corporate network and to that end identify the extra hardware resources required:

- Number of terminals: active, maximum
- Number of remote printers
- Volumes of transactions per week for main transactions
- Disk space in gigabytes
- Batch run times per week
- Volume of print in pages per week

Sizing rules-of-thumb

Develop a few 'rules of thumb' for ball-park sizing and budget costs, depending upon the exact environment:

- 2 mips per concurrent user on Unix
- 50 random disk file accesses per second on any hardware
- 1 to 2 weeks cost per function (such as 'main menu') for all aspects of development

5.7 Open Systems Standards

Open Systems is an IT strategy that promotes the idea of a freedom to choose between suppliers for all elements of producing, purchasing and running computer applications, networks and processors. This encourages competition and enables users to have a better choice of supplier for the acquisition of hardware, network (including the Internet), software and training.

The idea of open systems has lead to attempts to standardise hardware and software interfaces, rather than each manufacturer setting their own standards. One of the needs for instance is to be able to install systems and hardware which can all communicate, enabling users on a wide area network to access any system linked to that network.

In addition with 'open source' systems the source code is freely available with the package enabling users to tailor it to their own needs.

Open systems areas

There are advantages to be gained from compliance with open systems standards in the following areas:

- Application development environment
- Application transportability
- Hardware and operating system
- Internet
- Management reporting tools
- Network hardware and software
- Office automation software
- System software
- Training availability

Open software

When checking out software for its 'openness' consider:

- Availability of SQL in the DBMS and tools
- Availability under Unix versions
- Availability under Linux
- Availability under the various Windows versions
- Availability under X-Windows
- Database management systems available
- Management reporting tools available
- Open source availability if relevant

Open hardware

When selecting an open hardware platform consider the following:

- Machine performance
- Machine upgradability
- Ability for the platform to use multiple processors
- Recovery of database from failure
- Support for the system software on that platform
- Support for the application on that platform
- The past history of hardware compatibility for that supplier

5.8 Client-Server Issues

The client-server technique is where the desktop functions (the client) are separated from fileserver functions, improving system flexibility and data access. The Internet is an example of a client-server implementation. There may be a bias towards the function being more on the client, known as a 'fat client', or more on the server, known as a 'thin client'. There are advantages and disadvantages associated with using client-server techniques, some caution is needed and responsibilities need clarifying.

Client-server advantages

The advantages of using a client-sever configuration include:

- Users are presented with a familiar interface such as Windows
- There is increased user satisfaction due to the familiar user interface
- User productivity is increased for the same reason
- Users' access to data is improved through the use of management reporting packages
- On-going development is made more flexible due to separating out the functions
- Developer productivity is increased for the same reason
- Applications are more flexible for the same reason
- The user can always be presented with the latest versions of screens
- Desktop software can be integrated into the desktop interface
- Hardware costs are reduced by fitting functions to the hardware
- There is improved flexibility and scalability of hardware
- The server function can operate in parallel with the client function
- Overall performance may be improved
- Software licence costs are likely to be reduced

Client-server disadvantages

The disadvantages of using client-server include:

- There may be an impact on the network and central processor
- There may be high risk due to not being familiar with new technologies
- System management may take up extra time, particularly on the network
- There may be client-server skills shortages

5.9 Security Standards

Review the major risks when purchasing or providing an IT system to avoid costly data losses, business failure or a failure to meet legal obligations. Areas of risk include fraud, lack of control of change, unauthorised access to data, the input of faulty data, faulty systems, mis-operation of systems, lack of documentation leading to invalid alterations to the system, and failure to secure data against hardware and software failure. For each area of risk take action to protect the organisation and minimise the likelihood of disaster.

Security breach major risks

The risks involved in a potential breach of IT security include:

- Theft of essential equipment or data
- Disruption to the business process
- Physical interruption to the service
- External damage by viruses
- Unauthorised access
- Breach of confidentiality
- Failure to meet organisation and legal obligations
- Loss of integrity and quality of business data
- Fraud

Risk assessment and management

When assessing and managing the risks of IT systems:

- Assess the application and systems risks
- Assess the hardware risks
- Assess the risks of each link in the local and wide area networks
- Authorise the generation of all new employee and customer records via the appropriate person
- Authorise all orders/payments and split the order/payment process between two persons
- Authorise facilities in layers so that front line users have essential transactions only
- Authorise system and program changes via the appropriate persons including the user
- Avoid leaving individuals working on their own at a computer or terminal
- Challenge the identities of unknown people in office areas
- Change system identities on an irregular basis and don't email the new one
- Check assets to the asset register on a regular basis
- Encrypt sensitive data on the network such as user identities and passwords
- Ensure each person uses a unique user identity and password and keep them confidential
- For passwords avoid real names, dates of birth, reverse spellings, gradual changes
- Get internal or external auditors to review all systems, whether in-house or packaged
- Include the management of user identities, passwords and email in induction training
- Incorporate a firewall to other networks such as the Internet
- Involve audit skills in the specification and acquisition of new systems
- Limit access to computer areas and terminals
- Lock desks and offices when not in use
- Mark all hardware items with security codes and register them
- Mark leaver records immediately on all systems
- Minimise the movement of floppy disks and keep them secure since they are easily removed
- Never disclose passwords to anyone including the bank or police, especially over the phone
- Protect the network against message bombardment attacks, which might deny users a service
- Shred all unwanted documents
- Teach and encourage staff to carry out security checks
- Use a minimum of six alpha-numeric characters for passwords

Security training

When drawing up plans for security training:

- Include security in induction training
- Organise security training for all staff in the organisation
- Include Data Protection training
- Include security training in package and in-house systems user training
- Provide developers and administrators with good training on Windows NT, Unix, the network
- Emphasise the need for strict control of high-level passwords such as management and administration
- Emphasise the need to control individual user identities and passwords
- Provide training in the generation of passwords and remembering them
- Provide training in the sensible use of email and the avoidance of viruses

Security requirements specification

When specifying security requirements in a system consider the following:

- Put controls in place for access to the system and data
- Ensure only secure, accurate, valid data is accepted
- Ensure recovery from failures is easy, especially where high on-line availability is required
- Satisfy the requirements of auditors
- Produce an audit trails for key transactions
- Cover statutory requirements such as Data Protection and Government Agencies
- Put in change control to minimise data corruption & ensure projects are delivered to cost/timescale

Change control security

Incorporate security into change control:

- Encourage customers to specify the requirements and benefits of the change in writing
- Scope the impact, risks, timescales and costs of the change
- Ensure the customer formally accepts, defers or rejects the change
- Plan/re-plan the project if the change is accepted
- Draw up work agreements to formalise requirements and timescales
- Produce an implementation plan
- Carry out quality assurance testing
- Carry out user acceptance trials
- Agree formal operational releases with all customers and formally notify users

Testing security

Incorporate security into program and system testing plans:

- Prepare test data for each case
- Consider the effects of program changes
- Carry out systems testing
- Carry out quality assurance testing
- Assist users to carry out user acceptance trials
- Parallel run batch systems with existing systems
- Check and monitor pilot and fully-live runs

Operational release security

Incorporate security into the release of operational programs:

- Produce a final impact analysis
- Use a formal operational release notice
- Provide operational run sheets
- Carry out training of operational staff
- Back up operational programs, source code and data
- Inform users of the change
- Update the help desk arrangements

Documentation update security

Incorporate documentation version control for the following:

- System specification
- Program specifications
- Operating instructions
- Error recovery and restart procedures
- Administrators guide
- System user guide

Package evaluation security

When evaluating packages consider the package facilities against user requirements including data security:

- Evaluate packages strictly against a functional requirements specification
- Include security standards in the functional requirements specification
- Get suppliers to address security separately
- Include the supplier's response in the contract
- Evaluate user identity, password, access control security
- Evaluate file control security
- Check security through reference site visits
- Check security through acceptance testing

Data retention and recovery

Consider the security issues for data retention and recovery:

- Provide resilience through system version control
- Back up databases to external media
- Log all on-line transactions
- Make use of automatic rollback facilities if any
- Use off-site storage or fireproof safes for regular backups
- Carry out periodic testing of backups to ensure that they are effective
- Keep information for statutory periods, for instance financial year end for six years

5.10 Security in Systems

Build security into the whole environment to protect code and data. To do this ensure the integrity of the data, protect user identities and passwords, limit access to data to the level necessary, check batch input files for validity, check on data output, provide an audit trail of both on-line transactions and batch processes, and provide a secure program development environment.

Data safeguarding

Ways to safeguard data include:

- Back up data to external media
- Carry out automatic data reconciliation and balancing
- Carry out new/existing data validation by limiting type, range, via tables, cross-referencing
- Carry out software virus protection automatically by checking all incoming files, tapes, disks and all other external media, especially from the Internet
- Incorporate a firewall to the Internet to minimise unauthorised access and viruses
- Disallow users to view who is logged on, for example in Unix
- Enable auditing of data, transactions and systems; develop standard audit procedures
- Guard against hardware and software failure
- Incorporate on-line time-out with password re-entry
- Make use of check digits and hash totals to check the validity of reference numbers
- Make use of security cabinets and fireproof safes, off-site for archives
- Meet the requirements of the Data Protection Act
- Prevent fraud, disaster, damage, illegal access to data, user errors and operational errors
- Prevent unauthorised entry or access to data by users, programmers and operators
- Protect data against loss or corruption during storage, transmission and processing
- Restrict access to encryption keys to authorised managers
- Restrict physical access to areas to authorised personnel
- Use data encryption for sensitive data such as user identities, passwords, equal opportunities data
- Use the central fileserver for corporate data, not the local one

User identity and password security

Use the following security guidelines for logging into systems:

- Ensure the system cannot be accessed prior to entry of a valid user identity and password
- Encrypt user identities and passwords
- Ensure that software tools cannot bypass the checks or view the identity/password
- Disallow facilities to view or print passwords
- Allocate user identities uniquely to individuals
- Ensure that the user identity is unique, alphanumeric and at least five characters
- Ensure that passwords are not less that six alphanumeric characters, preferably eight
- Check the identity and password together and give a general failure message only
- Enable users to allocate their own passwords
- Prompt users for regular changes of passwords
- Discourage the use of names, dates of birth, telephone numbers and don't write them down
- Reject the use of cyclical passwords
- Deny the system administrator access to passwords
- Allow the system administrator to delete a password without knowing it
- Ensure that the system administrator deletes user identities as staff leave
- Enable the administrator to recognise unused identities and delete them
- Record the log-in and log-out times of all users
- Allow three unsuccessful log-in attempts only before clearing the identity and password
- On Unix disallow an initial log-in as 'root'
- Ensure that any encryption system is secure and split administration functions

Access level control security

When designing database systems enable facilities to be allocated to users' needs:

- Allow database read only, amend, insert, delete
- Allow individual application functions
- Allow access to specific parts of the data only

File controls security

When batch processing:

- Reject duplicate or incorrect input files
- Check the correct sequence of input files
- Ensure that files are received on time
- Check that all input records have been processed and check their total value

Printed output controls

To improve the security of printed output:

- Stamp the printed output with the date and time of production
- Visually check the printed output on a continual basis
- Compare control totals with those from earlier processes

Audit trails

To meet audit security requirements when accessing and amending databases:

- Allocate unique user identities to users and operators
- Provide an audit trail to cover the UK Companies Act
- Use audit trails to check who did what and when and ensure that they can't be directly amended
- Keep a check-sum on the audit trail to ensure there is no unauthorised amendment
- Record the user identity with the transaction (but not the password)
- Record the date and time of the transaction
- Record a sequential audit number with the transaction
- Record the nature of the transaction (insert, amend, copy, transfer, delete for example)
- Consider recording the information before and after changing
- Make use of audit inspection and analysis packages to carry out independent checks on the data
- Log batch processes carried out together with control totals

Program development security

When developing computer programs and systems:

- Test for valid and invalid sets of data when testing programs and systems
- Consider using live data as test data (but change personal names and addresses)
- Consider parallel running batch systems (deleting live data at the end)
- Insist that users carry out their own user acceptance testing
- Independently test the audit requirements
- Test recovery procedures
- Document security measures
- Consult operations staff at all stages
- Put change control into place

Access to source code security

Reduce the chance of unwanted changes being introduced to source code:

- Restrict access to program source code to authorised staff
- Formalise the release of operational programs
- Formalise the release of operating instructions and the job control language
- Formalise run sheets and any use of special versions of programs
- Secure source code and operational code archives
- Secure data archives
- Control authorised access to systems and copies of them

5.11 Data Protection Act

The 1998 Data Protection Act came into force on 1 March 2000. It sets out rules for processing personal information and applies to some paper records as well as those held on computers. The Act gives individuals certain rights. It also says those who record and use personal information must be open about how the information is used and must follow the eight principles of 'good information handling'. The 1998 Act is sufficiently different from the 1984 Act to require that all personal information systems be re-registered by October 2001.

The lists given below (except the last) are summaries reproduced with the kind permission of the Data Protection Commissioner. Detailed information can be obtained via the Data Protection Office help line on *01625 545 745* or via its web site at ***www.dataprotection.gov.uk***.

Data Protection principles

Anyone processing personal data must comply with the eight enforceable principles of good practice:

- Data must be fairly and lawfully processed
- Data must be processed for limited purposes
- Data must be adequate, relevant and not excessive
- Data must be accurate
- Data must not be kept longer than necessary
- Data must be processed in accordance with the data subject's rights
- Data must be secure
- Data must not be transferred to countries without adequate protection

Processing personal data

Personal data covers both facts and opinions about the individual. The definition of processing incorporates the concepts of 'obtaining', 'recording', retrieving', 'consulting', 'holding', 'disclosing', and 'use'.

Personal data will not be considered to be processed lawfully unless certain conditions are met:

- The individual has given their consent to the processing
- The processing is necessary for the performance of a contract with the individual
- The processing is required under a legal obligation
- The processing is necessary to protect the vital interest of the individual or to carry out public functions
- The processing is necessary in order to pursue the legitimate interests of the data controller or third parties (unless it could prejudice the interests of the individual)

Sensitive data

The Data Protection Act makes specific provision for sensitive data, which can include:

- Racial or ethnic origin
- Political opinions
- Religious or other beliefs
- Trade union membership
- Health
- Sex life
- Criminal proceedings or convictions

Processing sensitive data

Sensitive data can only be processed under strict conditions which include:

- Having the explicit consent of the individual
- Being required by law to process the data for employment purposes
- Needing to process the information in order to protect the vital interests of the data subjects or another
- Dealing with the administration of justice or legal proceedings

Paper files

The Data Protection Act covers information that is recorded as part of a 'relevant filing system', that is one in which the records are structured so that specific information relating to a particular individual is readily accessible.

Accessible paper records are broadly records for:

- School pupils
- Housing
- Social Services
- Health

Rights of individuals

The Data Protection Act 1998 extends the rights of individuals (data subjects) regarding their personal data:

- The right to subject access
- The right to prevent processing likely to cause damage or distress
- The right to prevent processing for the purposes of direct marketing
- The right in relation to automated decision-taking
- The right to take action for compensation
- The right to take action to rectify, block, erase or destroy inaccurate data
- The right to ask the Commissioner to assess whether the Act has been contravened

Telecommunications

Regulations implementing the provisions of the EU Data Protection Telecommunications Directive 97/66/EC came into effect with the 1998 Data Protection Act.

The Directive imposes special rules for the processing of personal data in:

- Public telecommunications systems
- Faxes
- Telephones
- Automated calling systems for unsolicited marketing

Criminal offences

There are a number of criminal offences created by the 1998 Data Protection Act and they include:

- Notification offences (such as failure to notify the Commissioner about personal data)
- Procuring and selling offences
- Enforced subject access (such as asking for access to data as a precondition to employment)

Promoting good practice

The duty to promote the following of good practice by data controllers is an important part of the proactive approach to the Data Protection Act.

For example clear ground rules are required to ensure employers' information practices are fair to employees particularly in relation to:

- Employee surveillance involving the collection of data, the interception of email or the use of CCTV for example
- Automated processing and decision-taking, using methods such as CV scanning and aptitude or psychometric testing
- Collection of new and sensitive data such as the results of alcohol or drug test results or genetic information

Data Protection practicalities

To help meet the Data Protection legislation:

- Make a person in the organisation responsible for Data Protection and ensure staff know who
- Train users in their Data Protection responsibilities
- Register all systems that record personnel data with the Data Protection Office
- Include the IT organisation's own systems where necessary
- Use the data for the registered purposes only
- Keep the data accurate and up-to-date
- Do not disclose personal information to enquirers without first establishing their right to it
- Know what you can and cannot disclose
- Retain data for the appropriate length of time only
- Use terminals and PCs sensibly and do not leave them logged on and unattended, including email
- Ensure that members of the public cannot see sensitive information on terminals and PCs
- Ensure that data is not lost or corrupted and back it up regularly
- Use passwords according to the organisation's standards including individual passwords
- Allow users to change their own passwords regularly including via automatic prompts

6. SYSTEM SPECIFICATION AND PRODUCTION

This chapter is concerned with in-house development and the production of tailored applications produced by software houses. Many of the issues are pertinent when purchasing packages.

The production of the system specification and estimating costs and timescales are dealt with. The chapter also covers system design, database design, on-line screen design, printed output, financial controls, process specifications, standard programs, coding standards and system implementation. It deals with the production of user guides, the provision of user training, the provision of maintenance and support services, and the management of requests for IT work.

6.1 System Specification

If the system is to be developed as a new system, either in-house or by a software supplier, produce a detailed system specification. Create the system specification from the functional requirements specification by the addition of samples of all screens, analyses, reports, broad processing details, database details and the implementation plan.

Include in the system specification only a manageable amount of detail, sufficient to inform the customer and analyst about the broad input, processing and output of the system, but leaving out the fine detail of the processing. Develop the document to become the long-term technical guide (but not a training document or user guide, which will need to be written separately, probably by the customer).

Use the system specification to derive accurate estimates of effort and cost, together with first guesses of timescales. In addition use the system specification for the basis of system and database design, agreeing and setting standards for on-line and printed layouts, and for financial controls and statistics.

System Specification contents

Develop the system specification from the functional requirements specification by adding:

- A breakdown of the system into sub systems if necessary
- Transaction names and their identities
- Screen examples integrated with the descriptions of on-line functions
- Field validation added to on-line functions
- Processing and decision tables added to on-line functions
- Report examples integrated with the descriptions of print functions
- Processing and program identities added to batch functions
- Implementations phases and timescales agreed with the user
- Database design details
- List of database record types and their descriptions
- System design standards and conventions to be incorporated into the system
- Data capture and cleansing details

6.2 Estimating Development Time

It will be necessary to estimate the potential cost of an in-house system at various stages. When a formal functional requirements specification or, better, a system specification has been produced, a fixed estimate can be given.

To be able to estimate the development costs, break down the project into smaller tasks. On-line transactions, batch functions and print schedules form a good basis for the breakdown. Ignore the experience of the development resources for costing purposes at this stage until tasks have been allocated to individual staff.

Allow five days for the development and testing of a simple on-line transaction or print schedule in a Fourth Generation Language, ten days for a more difficult one. Similarly, use five days for a simple batch transaction, ten or more days for a more complex one. It may be possible to produce many reports and analyses in much less time than this using a good report generator and one day per transaction may be more than sufficient. Double the development estimate to give the minimum effort for all elements of the implementation of the function. Vary this according to experience of the particular development environment.

Project time apportionment

Split the project up using the following suggested percentages for elements of the IT organisation's effort required, varying these percentages with experience and according to the particular circumstances:

Activity	Minimum %	Maximum %	Average %
Feasibility study	2	5	2.5
Investigation and analysis	5	15	10
Systems design & specification	10	20	15
System development	30	50	40
Package acquisition	5	15	10
Systems/acceptance trials	10	20	15
Implementation	10	15	12.5
Project management	10	15	10
On-going support per year	10	20	15

6.3 Project Timescales

Break projects down into activities and tasks as part of the project planning process and estimate the size and timescales of the tasks. Prioritise the various tasks to ensure the urgent ones are done first and seek the critical path to give the elapsed time for the project.

Project timescale weightings

When estimating the elapsed time for implementing a system take into account the skills of the development resources actually available and apply weighting factors to the original estimates:

Person	Weighting
Senior analyst/programmer	0.5
Experienced person	0.75
Middle experience	1.0
Inexperienced person	2.0
Trainee	3.0

6.4 System Design

If the system is to be developed in-house use the system specification as the basis for the design of the system, taking into account the need for system stability, long life and flexibility.

System design stages

The stages a project might go through during its design include:

- Identify the hardware options if this has not been done already
- Agree the preferred option with the project steering group
- Complete the design of the database
- Design and prototype transactions with an experienced user
- Finalise the system specification

System design aims

The aims to be achieved during system design include:

- Design screens to have a good interface with the user, that is make it user friendly
- Allow for both expert (fast ways of doing things) and occasional users (menus)
- Capture data once only at source and make best use of it
- Integrate the system into work procedures and avoid data input in batch later
- Produce good on-line response times and fast reporting and batch speeds
- Build in data security, system stability, recovery from failure of software or hardware
- Design to minimise maintenance and support and to enable support to be handed over
- Design to minimise minor enhancements
- Build in flexibility to cope with future enhancements
- Avoid the use of hard coding
- Design and code the system to be operationally stable and fail-safe
- Build in self-documentation with minimum support papers

6.5 Database Design

The use of a relational database is the preferred option. Keep the physical design of the database simple and flexible, especially if a hierarchical or network database is considered. Only hold data that can be captured automatically or can be kept up to date with certainty (there has to be a carrot for users to do this).

Database data design

When designing a database:

- Use a relational database if at all possible
- Allow one type of record only per database file
- Avoid the duplication of data
- Hold dates in the form **yyyymmdd**
- Make the names of fields, indicators and switches meaningful and document them
- Design for efficient data retrieval, both for standard and ad-hoc purposes
- Build in data access security
- Build in an audit trail with traceable transactions
- Build in data controls, that is make each file in the database self-balancing
- Use a standard format for tables
- Build in user help
- Build in flexibility and expandability for the future

Database standard files

Maintain a number of standard system files in addition to the application data such as:

- Customer organisation profiles (name, address, phone, fax, web and email addresses)
- User profiles showing permissions (transactions allowed, data areas allowed)
- On-line transactions details (including a description of the transaction)
- Tables file (include the table number in the code to simplify program look-up)
- Process history file (batch history, totals, statistics)
- Audit trail of on-line transactions, particularly those updating the database
- Help system

6.6 On-line Guidelines

Set standards for the following areas of on-line development, varying them to suit the development environment:

- Screen layouts
- User menus
- Dialogues with the user
- Security and access control
- Database definitions
- Database descriptions
- File names and extensions
- Transaction processing
- Reports
- Help system

Sign-on standards

Use the following sign-on standards for on-line transactions:

- Hide user identities and ensure that they are at least five characters
- Hide user passwords and ensure they are at least six alpha-numeric characters, preferably eight
- Allow users to alter their own password and force users to change password regularly
- If identity/password checks fail give a general error message only, having checked both first
- Disallow the viewing or listing of passwords
- Encrypt passwords and user identities in the database

User profile record

Include the following in user profiles:

- Operator identity
- Password
- Surname, initials
- Department
- Transactions, tables, actions, records and datasets (fields) permitted

Screen standards

Set standards for screens design to give a similar feel to all applications for the user such as:

- Put the system name at the top left of the screen
- Put the screen name at the top centre
- Put the screen identity at the top right
- Display prompts next to the bottom line
- Display error messages on the bottom left
- Display the current date, time, user initials bottom right
- Highlight data entry fields
- Highlight all fields in error in inverse, no sound, reporting first error only
- Use the same format for display and update
- Allow easy movement from display to update, given permissions
- For lists display up to 20 records per page and select a record by the cursor

Menus/commands standards

Consider the following when deciding how users will navigate around the system:

- Use menus with commands as an override
- Use commands of two or three character mnemonic or transaction number
- Consider optional parameters to commands such as record reference
- Allow users to temporarily or permanently move to another transaction

Help facilities

Consider the following when designing help facilities:

- Provide general system help
- Provide transaction level help
- Provide item level help
- Allow help descriptions to be user amendable

Property address standards

When designing screens (and forms) with postal addresses:

- Use the Post Office Address File (PAF) to generate addresses from the postcode/house number
- Use a standard display and update format
- Display (and print) the postcode and generate the postal walk number to get a postage discount

System parameters standards

To keep the system flexible allow authorised users to amend:

- All main system variables
- Help details
- Error report wording

Date standards

When designing systems with dates:

- Hold dates as **yyyymmdd** in the database
- Use the format **dd/mm/yyyy** for both input and output normally
- Interpret two digit years input or from the database for the millennium
- Consider whether a two digit year for output is acceptable

Table standards

When designing tables to hold codes and their descriptions:

- Use a short alpha-numeric code for a table entry and include the table number in the code
- Provide short and long descriptions for display purposes
- Allow 'insert', 'display', 'amend', 'delete', 'copy' actions
- Provide an easy way on update screens for users to look up codes and return them to the screen

6.7 Printed Output Standards

Consider using the following standards for printing, preferably via a standard print routine.

Schedule header standards

Print the following on a schedule header page:

- Customer name
- System name
- Program identity
- Schedule number and name
- Financial period number, date and time

Page header standards

Standardise the layout of headers on printed pages, for instance:

- System name
- Schedule number and name
- Program identity
- Financial period number, date and time
- Page number

Bar code standards

When printing bar codes to enable the easy re-use of reference numbers:

- Use bar code 128 (a common compact alpha-numeric code with control characters)

6.8 Financial Control Requirements

Ensure that suitable financial controls are built into packages and into in-house systems to act as controls within the system and to other linked systems, and to enable statistics to be derived.

Financial controls

Consider the following financial controls for systems:

- Hold a cumulative analysis of the major data records in the database
- Provide control reports of these and numbers and value of each type of transaction
- Make the system and files self balancing and part of the control report
- Provide a cumulative audit trail of financial (and non-financial) transactions
- Record the history of batch processes, with financial controls

6.9 Process Specifications

Use the system specification to derive the detailed process (program) specifications by expanding the system specification itself rather than creating yet another set of documents.

Process specifications strategy

When deciding on the strategy for program documentation:

- Don't have too many documents to maintain since they will get out of date
- For on-line transactions minimise detailed specifications (unless they are to be coded by trainees)
- Use the system specification and prototyping to build up transactions the customer is happy with
- Add the processing detail when the transaction format has been agreed
- Keep the outline of how the transactions function in the system specification
- Keep the detail of the processing in the coding (with annotation where necessary)
- Detail batch processes on paper more since there are fewer visual clues than on-line
- For batch processes document the links between transactions, programs and systems

Process specification format

Consider using the following layout for process (program) specifications:

- Process identification and name
- Context of the process (links to other processes)
- Input details and any screen or form layout
- List of functions performed
- Output required
- Error conditions in outline
- Test plan in outline

6.10 Standard Transactions and Programs

Make use of standard and skeleton coding rather than create everything from scratch. Standard and skeleton programs give the advantage of easy familiarisation so that anyone using the standard can understand the logic of almost any program quickly.

Standard transactions

Develop the following standard on-line transactions and use them in most systems:

- Application menus
- Audit trail
- Batch process history trail
- Calendar
- Organisation profile maintenance
- Error message maintenance (possibly user amendable)
- Help system (user amendable)
- Menu maintenance
- Organisation profile maintenance
- Printer identities
- Standard reports menu
- Tables maintenance
- Transaction list maintenance
- User log-on and security checks
- User data permissions checks
- User data permissions maintenance
- User profile maintenance

Skeleton programs

The following skeleton programs are examples that could be developed for the basis of on-line and batch transactions:

- Single record display and maintenance.
- Multiple record display and maintenance
- Multiple record browse and select record
- On-line run request process
- Batch extract
- Batch update
- Batch report

6.11 Coding Standards

Observe the following general points for program coding:

- Start from skeleton programs or similar previous programs
- Include a program summary at the start
- Use structured programming, but ensure that the main processing can be followed
- Number paragraphs in sequence
- Use meaningful paragraph names and descriptions
- Use meaningful data names
- Annotate switches and indicators
- Make use of tables for flexibility
- Put limited annotation throughout

6.12 Implementation Planning

Any project will go through a number of defined stages and here we are concerned with the final implementation activities following acquisition of the system, whether developed in house or bought in from a supplier.

Project stages

To recap, during system acquisition or development a project may go through many stages such as:

- Receive a request from a customer to consider the impact of a change
- Establish the terms of reference of the project and its scope
- Agree outline requirements
- Carry out a feasibility study
- Analyse the cost and service benefits arising from the project
- Report to management on the broad options
- Investigate the detailed requirements
- Produce and agree a functional requirements specification
- Carry out market evaluation of packages and self education
- Evaluate potential packages and suppliers
- Select the preferred supplier and a second choice
- Contract for the package
- Produce a system specification if a tailored solution is being considered
- Agree the system and database design for a tailored solution
- Produce the program specifications for a tailored solution
- Code and test programs for a tailored solution
- Present a prototype to users and management
- Produce a project implementation plan
- Produce and implement a quality assurance testing plan
- Assist the customer to carry out user acceptance trials to agreed criteria
- Finalise the detailed implementation plan
- Produce a user guide in conjunction with the customer
- Assist the customer or supplier to carry out user training
- Produce operational procedures
- Carry out batch parallel running on all of the data and reconcile differences
- Carry out pilot running on perhaps 5% to 10% of representative data
- Carry out phased live running and monitor the system
- Supply ongoing system support
- Carry out a post-implementation review

Implementation plan

When a particular solution to the business requirements has been agreed produce a detailed implementation plan, expanding any existing broad project plan, and agree it with the customer:

- Review Health & Safety requirements
- Carry out any necessary discussions with unions
- Assist the customer with Data Protection registration
- Determine the timescales envisaged by users
- Consult the original terms of reference
- Consult the functional/system specification formal agreement
- Determine hardware provision through capacity planning
- Determine network requirements through capacity planning
- Carry out enhancements to any existing hardware
- Determine and implement cabling and power requirements
- Determine software provision
- Carry out any tailoring of packages necessary
- Create the skeleton database
- Determine take-on requirements from existing data and data cleansing
- Determine the resources and expertise available in the customer organisation
- Determine the detailed implementation support required
- Devise a system benchmarking plan for on-line and batch
- Ensure that there is agreement of the system acceptance criteria
- Produce the users' operational procedures with the customer
- Review the on-line help with the customer
- Produce user and training guides with the customer
- Determine operational timetables with the customer
- Determine year-end operational requirements
- Provide input forms if any
- Provide output forms if any
- Produce operational control instructions
- Produce batch operating instructions
- Arrange supplier support and help line support
- Review system security requirements
- Organise database back-up arrangements
- Arrange for system recovery from hardware or software failure
- Produce back-up office procedures
- Produce disaster plans (often neglected)
- Assist with user acceptance trials using the functional/system specification and agreed criteria
- Carry out parallel running with the existing batch system and reconcile differences
- Arrange for post-implementation support
- Train the user's trainers and IT staff
- Assist the customer to carry out detailed training 'just-in-time'
- Phase the implementation of the live system, starting with a small typical area or module as a pilot
- Ensure that the chosen pilot tests as much of the system through to end
- Carry out pilot running on part of the data so that a manual recovery can take place if needed
- Review the success of the pilot live running
- Roll out the rest of the operational running
- Monitor and tune the operational system
- Carry out a full post-implementation review with the customer and get the system signed off

6.13 User Guide and Training

Part of the implementation of a project will be the production of a user guide (often by the users themselves) and training (often carried out by trainers identified from the users themselves).

User guide contents

The user guide for on-line transactions could be entirely on-line, with the ability to look up code lists in windows. The error descriptions should preferably be amendable by the customer's database administrator.

Describe each transaction in the user guide under the following headings, whether for packages or for in-house development:

- Transaction name
- Object of the transaction
- Screen or form layout
- Functions performed (input, processing, output)
- Field validation carried out and errors reported

Training users

Consider the following issues when training users in the use of new systems or new releases of existing ones:

- Identify users' training needs
- Take into account different user abilities and requirements
- Include security issues
- Include Data Protection responsibilities
- Agree the training plan and timetable with the customer
- Train just prior to implementation ('just-in-time')
- Identify a suitable training location away from normal work
- Produce a training guide (often best produced by the users themselves)
- Generate suitable training materials and handouts
- Check the availability of PCs, network and software
- Set up a suitable training database
- Notify trainees of the training timetable, location and agenda
- Obtain feedback on a standard form from the trainees on training completion

6.14 Maintenance and Support Provision

Following implementation of the system contact the customer to ensure that there are no major problems. This should include a visit to see the main transactions in use. Make support available to the customer by telephone for advice and for error reporting. With a large system queries and problems should be reported to the customer's central pool of expertise or help desk first.

Call log contents

Keep a log of faults and other calls, their current status and action taken, preferably by using help desk software.

Use the log to produce monitoring lists and analyses of calls for management and reporting purposes from the help desk database using a general management reporting package:

- Date and time of call
- Customer name
- System name
- Contact and phone
- Location
- Generated call reference
- Problem title
- Problem details
- Action taken
- Current owner of the problem
- Status of the problem
- Date problem due to be fixed
- Date problem fixed and checked
- Date customer notified of correction
- Date call closed

6.15 Work Management

Changes to systems or networks may be requested because of faults, shortcomings, lack of functionality, poor system performance, user improvements envisaged, changes in organisation policy, legislation, or new technical advances.

Get requests for work or scoping in writing and authorised by the appropriate customer. Use a standard format for work requests and make good use of IT to support the internal business processes involved. For substantial requests for work ensure that the user identifies the benefits, carry out an impact analysis and assist in the production of a report for management/steering group authorisation.

Log all requests for work or fault reports, whether actual or potential, and allocate those which can be authorised immediately to an analyst/programmer.

Work flow

When dealing with requests for work and with faults reported by customers use an IT system to control them:

- Receive work requests and faults from customers
- Prioritise work requests and faults
- Price work requests and get authorisation to continue
- Batch all associated work together and agree a timetable with the customer
- Schedule the work, balancing the work load and the skills available
- Keep the customer informed of progress
- Monitor the work production
- Analyse the work load for monitoring and reporting purposes

Work request contents

Devise a standard format for work requests on paper or better as part of an IT work management system:

- Customer name
- System name
- Title of the work request
- Date requested
- Outline requirements of the work request
- Benefits/cost-savings/reason for change
- Sponsor and phone
- Customer authorisation for work request
- Priority (high, medium, low)
- Timescale required and reason
- Work request reference
- IT organisation approach envisaged
- IT organisation estimated charges
- Date of estimate
- Date earliest completion
- Estimate acceptance by the customer
- Expenditure code if required (customer/system/contract/change)
- Work scheduled date
- Work completed date
- Date change authorised in the live system
- Date customer accepted the change

Work log contents

Summarise all logged work for costing/recharging and management reporting purposes:

- Customer name
- Contact and phone
- System name
- Title of work requested
- Date requested
- Action taken
- Date completed
- Value of work
- Type of work

Work specification and agreement

Specify work in summary form for experienced staff and include:

- Originator of the specification
- Project team work assigned to
- Person work assigned to
- Estimated effort in days
- Estimate of staff cost
- Date of the agreement
- Customer name
- System name
- Contact and phone
- Priority (high, medium, low)
- Date required
- Expenditure code (customer/system/contract)
- Change reference
- Work title
- Reference to any existing documentation
- List of main tasks required

Work checklist

Include a checklist at the bottom of the work specification for the analyst/programmer to record the action taken, with initials and dates for:

- Documentation updated
- Work completed and tested
- Quality assurance trials completed
- User acceptance trials completed
- New system version released and users notified
- New system version checked operationally

7. PACKAGES, TENDERS AND CONTRACTS

This chapter deals with the specification of the requirements for a package and its purchase where that is the preferred business option for an application. It covers the specification of the customer's requirements, gathering proposals from potential suppliers, the evaluation of packages, package benchmarking, package risk assessment, tendering and contracting.

7.1 Package Requirements

Prepare a specification of business requirements for the application before making any attempt to obtain quotations and use this to sound out the market and in tendering.

Application requirements

Specify the requirements of the package required formally, including:

- The various customer functions required, as in the functional requirements specification
- An easily tailored system
- Good system navigation
- Good administration facilities
- Fast on-line response time
- Interface to the Internet
- Batch run times acceptable
- Novice/experienced user facilities
- Users able to alter their own passwords
- Screens and prints legible
- User-defined fields/screens if required
- The customisation of screens and prints if required
- Audit trails incorporated
- Financial controls incorporated
- Archiving facilities including selective archiving
- Fiching and CD-ROM writing facilities
- Terminal printing facilities
- Pre-printed stationery facilities
- Compliance with the organisation's security standards
- Data Protection provisions, including data retention
- Standby facilities for when the system is down
- Help facilities
- Ease of migration to other software and hardware platforms

Package management reports

Specify the management reporting facilities required:

- Provide facilities for occasional users
- Provide facilities for expert users
- Provide fast standard management reports
- Provide fast ad-hoc reports
- Produce analyses, including cross-tabulation (matrix) reports
- Download to standard PC packages
- Provide good general functionality
- Allow reports to run in background mode
- Provide local printing facilities
- Provide central printing facilities

Open systems compliance

List the open systems requirements of a packaged solution:

- Application to be written in a hardware-transportable language
- Network to be an accepted standard able to link to other standards
- Hardware to be one of the Unix or PC Fileserver flavours
- Systems software to be standard for the flavour of hardware
- Standard SQL to be available for the DBMS and management reporting tools
- Office automation to run on the flavour of hardware and be able to link to applications
- Links into and from the Internet to be easily available
- Training to be available from a wide range of companies
- Consider 'open source' software in which the source code is freely available with the package

System support

List the supplier staffing and control issues that are essential to supporting a packaged solution:

- Ensure that there is a viable project plan and project management arrangements
- Include change control arrangements
- Consider the necessity and cost of any consultancy offered
- Assess the technical support available
- Review the data capture and data cleansing facilities
- Analyse the training to be offered
- Check the detailed implementation plan
- Ensure that there is post-implementation support available
- Review the documentation/user guide/on-line help quality
- Review the help line support available for office hours, out-of-hours, special runs, year end
- Ensure that there is a method of reporting and clearing errors and ensuring non-regression
- Consider the frequency and impact of software upgrades, documentation and cost
- Ensure that there is cover for new legislation in any contract and the cost
- Understand the account management arrangements
- Clarify support responsibilities and response times
- Ensure that there is adequate data security/disaster recovery support
- Understand the method of financing enhancements and user group support
- Consider whether BS5750/ISO9000 quality accreditation is necessary
- Clarify the support required from the user and IT organisations
- Understand how disputes will be resolved by arbitration

Data security and administration

Set out the data security arrangements required from the package:

- Use the organisation's security standards as the target
- Passwords must be encrypted and not visible to anyone
- Users must be able to change their own passwords
- Prompted password change must be standard
- User/password failures must be logged
- Menu/permissions maintenance should be easy
- There must be a single database view for application and tools
- Tools mustn't be able to bypass permissions
- Recovery from software failure must be possible
- Recovery from hardware failure must be possible
- Database roll-back should be the norm for recovery (but watch the overheads)
- Database restore and recovery should be exceptional
- The IT organisation should be able to tune the database, for example for reporting purposes
- Data import should be easy and secure
- Selective archiving should be possible
- Links to the Internet must be firewalled

Package sizing data

Identify the volumes of users and data to be supported by the system:

- Maximum concurrent and future potential on-line users
- Transaction rates required for the main functions
- Static data and dynamic data volumes
- Batch and print volumes

7.2 Package Proposals

Collect the details of proposals from potential package suppliers to meet the application requirements.

Supplier details

Identify the package supplier:

- Application name
- Supplier name
- Address
- Contact name
- Phone, mobile, fax numbers, email address

Package summary proposals

Summarise the package proposed by the potential supplier:

- Hardware and operating system
- Network and communications software
- Database management system
- Systems software
- Application programming language

Hardware proposals

Summarise the package hardware proposed:

- Processor, speed, memory
- Disk storage
- Terminals: concurrent, maximum, upper limit
- Printers proposed
- Conformity to open systems standards
- Resilience to software and hardware failure
- Growth potential

Network proposals

Summarise the package network proposed:

- Software identity and version
- Operating system proposed
- Configuration proposed
- Integration with the organisation's existing network
- Affect on the existing network
- Interface to and from the Internet
- Conformity to open system standards
- Resilience to software and hardware failure
- Software/hardware failure recovery
- Central and remote printing facilities
- Growth potential

Database proposals

Summarise the package database proposed:

- Software identity and version
- Database access security
- Software failure recovery
- Hardware failure recovery
- The impact of using a client-server version

Application software

Summarise the application software proposed for the package:

- The application name
- Language, version
- Application source and author
- Documentation available
- Age of the package
- Number of installations
- Limitations on number of users
- Site licence options
- Fit-for-purpose certification availability
- Frequency and method of new releases
- Source code availability
- Application software escrow arrangements

Package documentation

Summarise the package documentation proposals:

- User guide
- Operations guide
- Installation guide
- Technical guide

Technical staff availability

Summarise the supplier staff available to support the package:

- Number of staff available
- The expertise of the staff
- Whether there is reliance on single people

System performance

Summarise the on-line and batch performance of the package being proposed:

- On-line response time guarantees
- Batch run times
- Management report run times
- Ad-hoc report run times

Backup and recovery

Summarise the package backup and recovery procedures being proposed:

- The method of backing up the database
- Whether the system has to be taken down to allow back-up
- Method of logging transactions and its effect on performance
- Method of database recovery and system restart
- Likely recovery time

Package security

Summarise the package data security proposed:

- How well the package matches to the organisation's security standards
- Passwords must be encrypted and not visible to anyone
- Users must be able to change their own passwords
- Prompted password change must be standard
- User/password failures must be logged
- There must be an audit trail
- There must be built-in financial and numerical controls

Customisation and maintenance

Summarise the customisation and maintenance services being proposed for the package:

- Services provided such as consultancy
- Ease of customisation and change
- User customisation facilities

Package support

Summarise the support being proposed by the supplier for the package:

- The availability of help desk support
- Availability of knowledgeable staff
- Cover for out-of-hours, holidays, special runs, year end
- Method of reporting and diagnosing application faults
- Priorities for clearing faults and timescales

User friendliness

Summarise the general impressions of the interface to the user for the package:

- General user interface
- Novice and expert facilities
- Menu/transaction driven facilities
- Use of SQL and ease of use
- User help facilities

Package training

Summarise the training being proposed for the package:

- Application users, systems, operations
- Numbers of staff
- Duration of training sessions
- Location of training
- Documentation provided

Package licensing

Summarise the licensing arrangements being proposed for the package:

- Method of licensing and fees
- Possible discounts
- Maintenance costs
- Site/corporate licensing
- Installation costs
- Terms of new releases
- Warranty terms and duration of licence

User groups

Summarise any user group activity for the package:

- Number of organisations
- Current costs
- Services provided
- Method of proposing and funding enhancements

Reference sites

Summarise the reference sites for the package, preferably of your choice:

- Reference sites comparable to the organisation
- User base size at each site
- Database size at each site

Package installation

Summarise the method of installing the package:

- Method of distribution of the software
- Whether supplier or user installation
- Ease of installation
- Ease and frequency of upgrading

Package benchmarking

Summarise possible benchmarking for the package:

- Whether a user benchmark is possible
- Whether a 90-day trial with supplier assistance is possible

Implementation proposals

Summarise the implementation and project management arrangements being proposed for the package such as:

- Project management arrangements
- Project plan
- Education plan
- Training plan
- Data capture and cleansing
- Phases of implementation
- Parallel running of batch work
- Pilot running
- Full running
- Timescales

Package supplier viability

Investigate the viability of the package supplier:

- Financial viability via Companies House
- Time in business
- Company size
- List of successes and failures
- Experience of open systems
- Dedication to the product
- Assessment of user satisfaction
- Size of customer base
- Size of user base
- Approach to quality (BS5750/ISO9000)
- Technical experience
- Reliance on key staff
- Research and development investment
- Risk assessments of the product and the company

Package costs

Summarise the costs of the package:

- Consultancy costs
- Project management costs
- Hardware costs
- Networking costs
- System software costs
- Application software costs
- Office automation costs
- Training costs
- Implementation costs
- Running costs per year including hardware and software maintenance or rental, consumables
- Internal staffing costs
- Five year costs

7.3 Package Evaluation

Develop prioritised evaluation criteria on which to base judgements, deciding which criteria are essential and placing weightings against each criterion or group of criteria. At the end of the day it will be difficult to find a package that meets all needs.

If the main selection criteria are met it may be better to move the users' ways of working towards those of the best package rather than incorporate special tailoring. Tailoring will be expensive, difficult to maintain and probably unreliable since no-one else uses it. It will be better to influence the user group to incorporate new ideas into the package.

Package selection criteria

Develop criteria for the selection of a packaged solution to application requirements Score criteria results out of five, using weightings of one to three placed on each group of items to reflect the priority of functions and other criteria, and sum the final weighted scores.

Criteria for package selection might include all or some of the following:

- The core on-line and batch functionality, as in the functional requirements specification
- A proven and future-proofed operating system and network server
- Proven and future-proofed development environment
- Management reports and ad-hoc reports
- Interfaces to desktop users, other systems, the Internet
- Security and controls compared with the organisation's standards
- Millennium and European Monetary Unit compliance proven
- Support for user base, transactions and growth
- Reference sites of a similar size
- User base satisfaction feedback from questionnaires
- Active user group
- Response times for on-line and batch
- Local and central printing
- Connectivity of terminals over the organisation's existing network
- Local and wide area networks impact
- Impact on the network of a client-server version of the application
- Access to and from the Internet and firewalling
- Resilience to software and hardware failure
- Project plan viability and project management intentions
- Change management arrangements
- Training proposed
- Data capture and cleansing intentions
- Help desk, support, response times, key personnel arrangements
- Form of contract
- Payment plan linked to project plan milestones
- Risk assessment of the product and company
- Costs over five years

Package criteria weightings

The package acceptance criteria weightings could have the following meanings for functional features or groups of features:

Package feature importance	Weighting
Desirable feature	1
Fairly essential feature	2
Very essential feature	3

Package match scores

The package criteria matching scores could have the following meanings:

Comparison of package with requirements	Score
Requirements not met at all	0
Very poor match, not really acceptable	1
Barely adequate match	2
Reasonable match	3
Good match	4
Excellent match and most requirements met	5

Package user base questionnaire

Contact a selection of users of the package from similarly sized organisations and document the findings:

- System, user, contact, phone
- User sites sizes and data volumes
- Number of existing on-line users
- Length of time from placing order to first phase and to last phase
- Was there a good match with functional requirements?
- Does the application supplier have a good knowledge of the subject?
- Was much tailoring of the package necessary?
- Was the software delivered on time?
- Was the system error free when delivered?
- Were any errors cleared quickly?
- Did any error regression occur in later releases of the system?
- Was training satisfactory?
- Was data capture and cleansing successful?
- Was implementation successful?
- Is the on-line system response time good?
- Is the speed of management reports good?
- Is the speed of ad-hoc reports good?
- Is the speed of batch runs satisfactory?
- Is the use of a help line successful?
- Is technical support available?
- Was the project managed well?
- Do all stakeholders think that the system is fit for its purpose?
- Is the system good value for money?
- What were the staffing implications?
- List of in-house contacts: End Users, IT Support, Audit, Accountants

7.4 Package Benchmarking

Package benchmarking is expensive both from the supplier and the user point of view and should be avoided if at all possible. Standard benchmarks exist and may be a guide if the supplier has produced them for that package running on particular software and hardware.

Instead of benchmarking at the selection stage find a reference site of a similar size and configuration and develop acceptance criteria to be measured during pilot and final running. Benchmarking is essential however during the implementation phase.

If the evaluation of a package, however, must include an in-house benchmark with support from the potential supplier, organise the following stages:

Benchmark evaluation plan

Develop a benchmark plan in consultation with the package supplier:

- Agree an evaluation plan and timescales with all management and the supplier
- Set up project management arrangements
- Estimate and identify the user and IT resources needed to carry out the evaluation
- Identify the software supplier's resources and costs
- Identify the hardware resources required
- Agree on a location with suitable hardware and software to carry out the evaluation
- Develop the evaluation criteria (based on the functional requirements specification)
- Capture or generate a suitable database
- Produce on-line and batch test data
- Produce the on-line and batch simulation scripts required
- Organise the staff training required
- Carry out on-line benchmarking
- Carry out batch benchmarking
- Re-benchmark during the pilot project

Package acceptance criteria

Develop criteria for the acceptance of a package during its initial phase of implementation, whether or not an independent benchmark is carried out:

- Develop the acceptance criteria and test conditions with the user
- Allocate sufficient senior staff and time to carry out the tests
- Set up a large database and network representative of operational data, users and conditions
- Document the tests to be carried out and the expected results
- Set up a mechanism to feed shortcomings back to the supplier

7.5 Package Risk Management

When considering the purchase of a package (or in-house development) identify the risks and classify them as high, medium or low and decide how those risks will be managed (also see 'risk assessment').

Package risks

Risks associated with packages include:

- Access to the system from existing networks may be a problem
- Benefits or potential achievements of the system may be exaggerated
- Client-server issues may cause load problems
- Connectivity of existing terminals may be a problem
- Contract/service level agreement may be poorly defined
- Core application functionality fails to meet the requirements
- Costs of hardware, network, training, consultancy, project management, licences, interfaces, data capture, tailoring, may be hidden
- Data capture/conversion/cleansing may be poor
- Database environment may be non-standard or may fail to meet the specification
- Development environment may be non-standard
- Graphical user interface may cause too high a load compared with a text interface
- Implementation fails to be properly planned and managed
- Interfaces to other systems may be a problem
- Lack of a cost-benefit analysis
- Lack of in-house project management expertise
- Loss of the developers of the package
- Management reporting tools don't come up to expectation
- Operating system and fileserver environment may be a problem
- Over-reliance on advice and cost predictions from suppliers
- Package has an adverse load on the existing network and hardware
- Resilience to software and hardware failure may be poor
- Response times across the network may be unacceptable
- Security and controls may be inadequate
- Specification of user requirements may be inadequate
- Supplier expertise in some areas may be lacking
- Support from the supplier may be inadequate
- The package may not be a proven solution
- Training quality is not up to expectation
- User base may be too small to prove the package
- User group activities may be ineffective
- User resources required are underestimated

Risk management

Manage risks associated with packages as follows:

- Involve representatives of all stakeholders in the project
- Determine essential requirements
- Provide a proper business case including a cost/benefit analysis
- Produce a functional requirements specification
- Evaluate all options to business requirements
- Use standard products and find a similar user site
- Use a recognised project management methodology
- Ensure that there are sufficient resources from all sides
- Communicate progress to the management of all parties
- Investigate the likelihood and impact of risk occurrence
- In the first instance avoid risks
- Transfer risks to someone else who can deal with the risk better
- Accept risks if they are small
- Control risks and prepare contingency plans
- Carry out a continual review of risks during the life of the project or system

7.6 Tender Questionnaires

Consider the use of a tender questionnaire to find out details of companies and whether they are interested in tendering for, and capable of supplying, the required product. Then go out to tender based on a restricted list of vetted potential suppliers.

Company details

Document the details of the companies interested in tendering:

- The name of the company
- Address for correspondence
- Named contact, position, phone, mobile and fax numbers
- Registered office address
- Type of company (sole trader, partnership, private limited, public limited)
- Names of directors, partners, company secretary
- Details of any involvement in any firm that has been liquidated or gone into receivership
- Details of any employment of the company by the organisation
- Details of any of any company relations to the organisation's senior management
- Involvement in other firms who provide services to the organisation

Technical references

Technical references of the company interested in tendering:

- Details of any deductions for damages in respect of any contract within the last three years
- Details of any contract terminated under the terms of the contract
- Details of any contract not renewed due to failure to perform to the terms of the contract
- Details of any damages awarded against the firm in respect of any break of contract in the last three years
- Details of any award made against the firm by a tribunal or court dealing with employment matters in the last three years
- Details of any industrial action taken against the firm in the last three years

Contract references

Details of similar contracts won by the company interested in tendering:

- Contract title
- Name, address, organisation
- Contact and phone
- Type of work
- Capital or annual value of work
- Contract type (such as fixed cost, commission)
- Start and end dates of contract

Contracts previously won

Details of similar contracts with the organisation won by the company interested in tendering:

- Contract title
- Department
- Contact name and phone
- Type of work
- Capital or annual value of work
- Contract type (such as fixed cost, commission)
- Start and end dates of contract

Contract guarantees

Details of contract guarantee schemes offered by the company interested in tendering:

- Name of organisation or scheme
- Registration or membership number
- Value of work guaranteed
- Date of expiry of membership

Financial information

Financial details of the company interested in tendering:

- Person responsible for financial matters
- Name and address of banker
- Audited company accounts within the last 12 months including balance sheet, profit and loss, directors/auditors report
- Details of any outstanding claims or litigation against the company
- VAT registration number

Liability insurances

Public, Employers and Contractors Liability insurances held by the company interested in tendering:

- Insurers
- Policy numbers
- Extent of cover
- Expiry dates
- Copies of the policies

7.7 Tendering

Having familiarised oneself with the market in the area of the required purchase organise the tendering process, including the finalisation of the specification of requirements and the timescales envisaged, using the assistance of a small panel of interested parties.

Tender process organisation

Manage the tendering process:

- Keep an audit trail of actions taken and results
- Organise a small representative group to form a panel
- Ensure the panel has the required skills including application, IT, purchasing, financial and auditing
- Agree the responsibilities of the panel
- Agree the timetable for the tender process
- Use standard forms of tender questionnaire/tender/contract
- Follow the organisation's standard procedure for tendering
- Decide if it will be necessary to advertise in the European Journal

Tendering timetable

Organise and agree the whole tendering timetable:

- Date by which potential suppliers will be invited to express an interest
- Questionnaire deadline (for a restricted tender)
- Advertisement date
- Deadline for tender queries
- Tender deadline date and time
- Tender evaluation dates
- Date for selection of the preferred supplier

Tender invitation details

When drawing up a tender invitation consider using a tabular format with room for potential supplier responses to criteria on the right:

- Use the functional requirements specification for the basis of the tender
- Produce a comprehensive specification to avoid an inability to compare tenders
- Avoid follow-up questions by using a comprehensive specification
- Ask suppliers to tender in a standard format to make comparison easier
- Ask for a model of part of the system if necessary and feasible
- Request reference sites of a similar size
- Enclose the organisation's security standards
- Outline the open systems conformity required
- Outline links with other systems, real-time and batch
- Request details of systems and networking software
- Request details of database software and its use of standard SQL
- Outline the support services required
- Outline the implementation support expected
- Outline the training requirements, location and method
- Request details of documentation available for support purposes
- Outline the hardware and network considerations
- Stipulate the system performance requirements and how that will be tested
- Stipulate the system availability and resilience requirements
- Indicate the project management arrangements intended
- Request details of software warranty and maintenance
- Request details of any certification available for the software
- State the broad selection criteria to be used (but not the weightings)
- Indicate the key success factors and acceptance testing to be performed
- Request details of any of the organisation's accommodation, facilities and staff required
- Request details of the potential supplier's staffing for the project
- Outline the contract monitoring to be carried out
- State the costs summary format required

Tendering procedures

Indicate the formal tendering procedures to the potential supplier:

- Give the project's name and an outline description
- State the tender closing date and time
- Indicate where tenders are to be returned
- Outline the format of the tender and the number of copies required
- Give contact names and phone numbers for technical, application, administration queries
- Indicate the tender opening procedure and the method of evaluation
- Include Health & Safety conformance
- Outline any environmental factors that may be involved
- Outline the quality assurance expected from the supplier
- Outline the likely contract termination conditions
- Request details of similar work done in the past, being done now and being bid for
- Outline the draft contract terms and conditions
- Consider including the organisation's standard form of IT contract as guidance
- Include a tender invitation disclaimer re 'no commitment to accept any tender'
- If necessary, include a glossary of terms

Tender selection process

When preparing for the evaluation of tenders:

- Ensure that the evaluation process has been organised before the tenders return
- Organise formal tender opening by an independent body such as auditors or solicitors
- Pass the tenders to the original panel for evaluation
- Get incomplete responses sorted quickly in writing
- Check that tenders are arithmetically correct and complete
- Use random selection to reduce the shortlist if necessary
- Interview the suppliers posing the same questions if necessary
- Check on potential suppliers through the reference sites given
- Review the tender strategy if there has been a poor response

Tender evaluation

When evaluating tenders:

- Check and document the potential supplier's details
- Use the 'most economically advantageous tender' unless there is good reason
- Use input, process or output evaluation criteria, preferably output
- Consider a mixture of input and output criteria
- Use weightings against criteria to reflect more essential requirements
- Check the tender functionality proposed against the requirements specification
- Identify application and technical experience and the company's capacity to support
- Evaluate technical support and training proposed
- Understand the quality and performance intentions of the company
- Check the proposed project implementation plan for viability
- Ensure all elements of cost are covered by the price
- Select the preferred supplier and a standby
- Communicate the results to all of the potential suppliers and to management

7.8 Contracting

The following paragraphs summarise advice on selecting and contacting with a package supplier.

Suppliers and their products

When considering suppliers, their products and their services:

- Go for risk sharing with the supplier
- Consider popular products since these will have better support and a better life span
- Stick to your specification and selection criteria
- Decide whether the company understands and is committed to the product and is stable
- Visit a reference site that uses the same application version, and one which fits your criteria rather than the supplier's
- Don't accept suppliers' benchmarks without analysis and practical proof
- Conduct an independent benchmark if only during pilot running and final implementation
- Link the payment profile to milestones in the project implementation plan

Contract contents

Preferably tie any application contract in with the supply of the hardware to avoid arguments about who is responsible if there are response time or throughput problems with the system.

Having selected a preferred supplier and a standby use a standard form of contract suitable for IT:

- Use the organisation's standard form of contract if possible, rather than the supplier's, or use both
- Involve the organisation's legal department in the process
- Incorporate the organisation's financial regulations if any
- Detail the intended software supply, including systems software
- Specify the level of software maintenance and enhancements
- Include supplier services such as project management, consultancy, training, data capture/cleansing
- Include any expenses
- Detail hardware supply including networking
- Tie in the supply of application software to the supply of hardware
- Specify the level of hardware maintenance needed
- Specify the system performance expected
- Include a technical specification covering benchmark and sign-off criteria
- Document the acceptance testing to be carried out
- Attach an outline project plan
- Agree a payment plan linked to the milestones in the project plan
- Agree the action to be taken on failure to supply to the quality and time expected
- Include the conditions for contract termination
- Outline the method of dealing with any contract variations
- Include the functional requirements specification as an appendix
- Don't forget the sanity clause!

8. STAFF MANAGEMENT

This chapter deals with human resources, which includes the management of both staff and one's own career. Generally, managers should concentrate on carrying out their management functions, and not get involved in detailed work, which may lead to neglect of some duties, particularly those disliked.

The chapter outlines the functions of a manager, team leadership, stress recognition and management, grievance and disciplinary procedures, team management, and staff development and training. It also covers staff appraisals, recognising managers' competences, upwards appraisal and the recruitment of staff. Issues concerned with one's own career include job hunting, managing oneself and socialising.

8.1 Management Functions

Management of the various operational areas covers planning activities, organising the execution of those activities, providing direction and guidance for staff and controlling and reporting on the activities. Management duties also include deciding on strategic direction, providing a safe working environment, managing staff, managing the customer relationship and monitoring the performance of the organisation.

Management methods

There are various approaches to management and it will be appropriate to use a combination according to the circumstances:

- Management by delegation by providing information, resources and support, backing decisions and feedback
- Management by objectives by agreeing goals and monitoring progress against them
- Management auditing by analysis of the effectiveness of work outcomes
- Management by exception by receiving brief reports except when there are problems
- Management by budget monitoring
- Performance appraisal through an analysis of successes and failures
- Ratio analysis over a period of time by comparing two key indicators such as sales against bad debts
- Standard costing whereby actual costs are compared with estimated costs

Management functions

Management functions include:

- Deciding on strategic direction for the organisation and gaining support for it (see Chapter 2)
- Providing and maintaining a healthy and safe working environment for employees
- Providing direction to staff
- Forecasting future staffing needs, recruiting and dismissing staff
- Evaluating and developing staff and negotiating pay or other rewards
- Managing customer relationships
- Planning activities and the use of resources
- Organising the execution of the activities
- Controlling and reporting on the activities
- Evaluating the organisation's overall performance and quality

Operational areas

An IT manager may control one or more of the following operational areas:

- Administration
- Customer care and standards
- Finance
- Help desk
- Marketing
- Operational production
- Personnel
- Purchasing
- Requirements analysis and system acquisition/production
- Sales
- Stores and assets

Management planning activities

Management planning activities include:

- Forecasting work
- Scheduling work
- Setting standards for work
- Planning projects
- Staffing projects
- Setting targets for staff
- Planning materials
- Planning facilities
- Planning the budget
- Deciding what internal management reports are required
- Reviewing old systems on a regular basis

Organising projects

When organising projects as a manager:

- Define and agree the objectives of the project or organisation
- Identify and analyse the activities needed to achieve the objectives
- Break down the activities into measurable tasks
- Allocate staff with the appropriate skills to carry out the tasks
- Obtain agreement from managers on achievable goals for the tasks
- Provide for the management and co-ordination of the activities
- Establish communication and reporting meetings

Decision making skills

All managers are continually having to make judgements and it is useful to consider how best to prepare for critical decisions:

- Ensure the decision is your problem; otherwise pass it to the appropriate person
- Allow sufficient time for decision making and agreement
- Consult with those affected before and during making decisions
- Understand the problem, the reason and the type of decision needed
- Research to see if the problem has occurred before
- Decide what are the issues and prioritise them
- Decide what are the key objective criteria for the decision
- Break down the problem into smaller elements
- Gather and analyse information to enable a decision to be made, including from databases
- Consider options to solve the problem and precedents
- Assess the risks and impact of each option and how they can be dealt with
- Eliminate unacceptable options and keep other options open
- Take advice on difficult decisions and consider how to deal with worst cases
- Occasionally it may be useful to 'leave options open'; that is postpone the main decision
- Decide on the safest and the best option and agree persons to implement it and the timescales
- Consider how to deal with any risks by preparing a contingency plan
- Make decisions known to management and staff as soon as possible
- Justify decisions, usually in writing, certainly in note form for future reference
- Implement the preferred option, involving those affected
- Monitor the results, review the decision in the light of the results, and learn lessons

8.2 Politics in Management

It is essential to understand the politics of the whole organisation, to use good politics in dealings with others and to discourage bad politics:

Good politics

Use good politics in dealings with the organisation:

- Identify stakeholders, decision-makers and their leaders
- Form good relationships with the stakeholders and decision makers
- Keep the stakeholders and decision makers informed
- Reconcile stakeholders' issues with those of the decision makers
- Disclose the appropriate information to stakeholders
- Make deals of mutual benefit to both sides

Politics to be stopped

Discourage bad politics both within the IT organisation and within the whole organisation:

- Discourage secret meetings
- Avoid asking for and carrying out favours
- Avoid hidden decisions
- Don't argue through official memos (it's better to meet, phone or email)
- Avoid passing the buck
- Discourage the open criticism of colleagues, especially to or in front of customers
- Stop rumours circulating

8.3 Team Management

Team managers are responsible for the delivery of services and for the staff involved and are facilitators for their teams. Team management involves regularly analysing, prioritising and planning the work in hand and potential new work. It also means keeping the team busy by scheduling and agreeing workloads, giving the appropriate feedback to staff, monitoring progress against targets, reporting on the progress of tasks by staff and analysing the work done for management reporting purposes.

Resource planning

When planning the use of staff resources:

- Document the work in hand and already authorised (whether new work, enhancements or support)
- Estimate the resources required for each job, staff involved and percentage of their available time
- Document the free resources still to be scheduled
- Consider and list any other potential work that may arise or needs to be sought

Work scheduling and monitoring

When planning and scheduling work for staff:

- List and prioritise the work to be allocated and determine the timescales
- Plan the allocation of work according to who is free and the skills required to do the job
- Share interesting and routine work, and provide opportunities
- Clearly define what is required, prioritise it and agree deadlines preferably in writing
- Go over the work with the individual rather than sending a message
- Supervise and monitor the work to ensure quality and timescales
- Keep yourself freed up to do the manager's job properly

Feedback handling

When giving feedback to staff on work:

- Give feedback early to enable action to be taken
- Ensure feedback is clear, accurate, specific, concise but usable
- Be positive to reinforce good practice
- Go over work methods rather than personal issues
- Avoid direct confrontation except as a last resort
- Use negative feedback to correct bad behaviour, but don't be destructive
- Sandwich unpleasant feedback between positive feedback

Staff report contents

Produce formal staff target progress reports monthly consisting of:

- The person involved
- Targets agreed with timescales
- Percentages of targets expected
- Percentages of targets achieved
- Comments

Work analysis

Analyse work done by individual members of the team and the team as a whole for the current month and cumulatively for the year for type of work. Produce resource planning reports monthly, consisting of weeks estimated for the next six months, using 75% to 80% loading for staff to allow for staff overheads including leave and sickness.

Types of work could include:

- Support for existing systems
- Clearance of faults in existing systems
- Legislation/minor enhancements to existing systems
- Investigation of potential new projects
- Projects authorised by management and being implemented
- Overheads such as leave and sickness

8.4 Team Leadership

Good team leadership is about developing specific leadership skills. Clear thinking and analysis, motivating staff and managing their performance are paramount. Dealing with inefficiency and the causes and effects of stress are also vital. It is important to provide opportunities for staff by delegating appropriate work.

Leadership attitude

Use the following leadership guidelines:

- Abandon old methods of working if they are no longer relevant and try new ones
- Be good at managing marketing
- Be good at oral and written communications
- Be good at planning and the control of plans
- Be motivated by achievement
- Be reliable and adaptable
- Be willing to involve and encourage others
- Believe in yourself and your staff
- Build the team and work as part of the team
- Deal with conflict, bad news or unpleasant issues
- Deal with financial, project and contract management
- Establish and encourage high standards
- Generate enthusiasm
- Have a belief in the projects in hand
- Have a positive attitude
- Have the imagination to see opportunities
- Manage change well
- Manage staff well
- Network with contacts
- Organise and motivate yourself and others
- Provide a role model for other staff

Leadership actions

Take the following actions as a leader:

- Build relationships with influential people and other teams
- Communicate relevant issues to staff
- Deliver promises and don't promise things that can't be delivered
- Develop an ability to determine strategic direction and objectives
- Discuss successes and new ideas
- Encourage team members to support each other
- Keep team members fully occupied to free up yourself to manage
- Make clear confident decisions after time for thought and consultation
- Produce management reports that are tailored, well-presented and timely
- Provide staff and management with the reports and feedback they need, but don't overload them
- Recognise that others may have good ideas and support them
- Re-plan the provision and use of staff, finance and materials resources on a regular basis
- Show a willingness to take risks when they have been properly assessed
- Show integrity and understanding to encourage colleagues to have faith in you
- Walk about work areas occasionally and see all operations in action

Motivation of staff

It has been said that people have five basic needs: physiological (food, clothing, shelter, etc), safety, social, esteem and self-fulfilment.

Keep these needs in mind when deciding how to motivate staff, remembering that only some of these are provided by a salary:

- Consider following the standards for 'Investors In People'
- Provide pleasant working conditions and re-decorate fairly frequently
- Persuade and guide staff rather than force them to carry out work
- Get team commitment to the main tasks in hand and the deadlines required
- Share enthusiasm for jobs with staff and keep promises
- Share interesting and uninteresting work and rotate staff
- Keep staff busy but happy to avoid loss of drive and interest
- Set demanding but achievable targets for the team and for individuals
- Set and agree tasks, priorities and timescales with the team and individuals
- Carry out formal monitoring against team and individuals' targets
- Give non-financial rewards including a hand-written note, training, equipment
- Counsel team members if problems occur
- Take early steps to avoid and resolve conflict
- Accept and give constructive criticism whilst remaining calm
- Agree corrective action to problems
- Be friendly, reasonable, honest, clear, show trust
- Socialise with the team and treat them to lunch occasionally
- Allow some relaxation during working hours so long as targets are met
- Develop, publish and monitor standards and guidelines
- Keep staff informed, but don't overload them with information
- Watch for lack of motivation causing absenteeism
- Pay the appropriate salary and provide good working conditions

Staff Management

Empowering staff

To spread workloads, to enable experience to be gained and to give the best service to the customer:

- Design jobs to enable staff to use their skills and obtain satisfaction
- Ensure managers have the appropriate leadership skills and training
- Position the manager's work space close to the team to enable support to be given
- Make sub-managers accountable and be clear about their duties
- Involve sub-managers in the whole management of the team
- Empower staff to take opportunities and set themselves stretching tasks
- Involve team members early on in planning, and explain how jobs fit into the overall picture
- Allocate suitable work to staff according to their abilities, but allow staff some initiative
- Ensure that a task is owned and completed by one person
- Hold short regular team meetings on projects' progress
- Provide formal reports to management on staff resource planning and progress
- Hold weekly meetings with individuals and give constructive comments on progress
- Praise staff and the team where work has been done well and targets met
- Provide feedback on performance and help analyse failures and action to be taken
- Display team progress in graphical form and update at least weekly
- Encourage staff to be part of the team and support them
- Encourage the discussion of ideas within the team for improving the business processes
- Carry out both regular and irregular appraisals and discussion of career progression
- Ensure that there are opportunities for career development
- To develop skills provide support and guidance, and formal and informal training
- Consult with and brief team members on decisions and changes affecting them
- Circulate relevant bulletins including the work done by the whole organisation and staff
- Use IT to improve communications, for example mailing lists

Delegation of work

When considering staff workloads:

- Plan your own work to use your particular skills
- Delegate routine and less critical tasks to concentrate on the main issues
- Delegate work to staff according to their ability, discussing first in draft form
- Delegate specialist tasks to those who have the skills or need to develop them
- Explain what work needs doing, why, priorities, costs, resources and the date it's needed
- Put delegated work in writing to avoid misunderstandings, but leave scope for initiative
- Inform staff of the authority they have for decisions and what needs to be referred back
- Explain how you will guide and monitor them and what reports are expected back and when
- Don't interfere unnecessarily, but have contingency plans and keep customers informed
- Delegate budgetary responsibilities to appropriate managers
- Log delegated work, monitor progress and the success of the delegation process
- Ask people who raise issues to suggest solutions to those issues

Performance management

To improve the work performance of staff:

- Analyse strengths, weaknesses, opportunities and threats
- Maximise strengths and opportunities by building on them
- Minimise weaknesses and threats by setting goals to address them
- Develop problem-solving and decision-making skills
- Carry out regular staff reviews to help with career development
- Compare actual project costs, income and performance with estimates and take action if necessary
- Carry out regular audits of the operational procedures of the organisation

Inefficiency management

When inefficiencies with staff have been identified:

- Document the problems and approach the person with the facts
- Go over the problems with the person and spell out the impact
- Possible impacts will include the effect on customers and other staff
- Make the position clear, but offer help; don't allow the employee to bluff
- Identify the causes such as poor direction, laziness, distractions, lack of motivation, overwork, personal problems, lack of loyalty, lack of time management, lack of prioritisation or stress
- Concentrate on dealing with objective issues rather then emotional ones
- Consider short and long-term solutions including moving the person to another area
- Consider training, coaching and job redesign
- Tackle lazy staff by setting mutually agreed deadlines on a weekly basis or daily if necessary
- Eliminate underachievement to avoid the business being affected

Difficult staff

There are going to be lots of reasons for having to cope with difficult staff, humans being what they are:

- There may be personal, psychological or cultural problems as the root cause
- Ways to deal with them must be found to avoid affecting other staff and the business
- Use first name terms to help with the relationship
- Get to know how to handle specific people by understanding how they respond best
- Give any warranted attention and praise to reinforce good work
- Monitor their work closely and consider discipline for poor behaviour

8.5 Stress Management

Stress causes poor productivity and needs to be recognised through the symptoms displayed, whether in oneself or in others. The causes need to be identified and action taken to relieve the stress.

Stress symptoms

Some of the symptoms of stress in oneself or in others are:

- Aggressive behaviour
- Complaints about work quality
- Erratic behaviour
- Excessive use of medicines
- Fatigue
- Fed up with life
- Frustration over failure to get results
- Full diary for weeks ahead
- Full in-tray and an inability to deal with it
- Going home late consistently and working extra hours
- Headaches
- Ill-prepared for meetings
- Inability to set and follow priorities
- Increased sickness and absence
- Increased smoking
- Increased staff turnover
- Increased use of alcohol
- Insomnia
- Irritation with colleagues
- Loss of confidence in oneself
- Loss of memory or concentration
- Low productivity
- No time for holidays
- Not taking exercise
- Not taking part in domestic or social life
- Over-emotional behaviour
- Personality clashes
- Taking work home
- Unkempt appearance
- Unwillingness to discuss problems

Stress causes

The basic causes of stress may be:

- A conflict of interests
- External issues such as domestic problems
- Job insecurity or status or career
- Lack of clarity of work requirements
- Not coping with change
- Poor job description
- Poor management
- Relationship problems
- Too much responsibility
- Working conditions
- Workload

Stress management of staff

When stress in an employee has been recognised:

- Analyse the cause of the stress and find ways to change it
- Avoid situations that cause stress, such as personal conflict
- Consider moving the person to other areas or duties
- Use appropriate staff to counsel the employee
- Clarify job roles to avoid ambiguity
- Provide training in management techniques
- Empower employees in the appropriate roles they can cope with
- Set and agree realistic priorities and targets
- Appraise strengths and weaknesses, and deal with weaknesses
- Allow discussion of problems when appraising staff
- Let people know they are valued
- Motivate others through good practice and coaching
- Discourage a culture of staying late at work or taking work home
- Be flexible with staff with other responsibilities

Stress management of oneself

Find ways of reducing stress in oneself:

- Don't try to be perfect
- Limit the number of tasks taken on and complete some before taking on others
- Don't take on workloads that can't be coped with
- Don't take on other people's problems
- Use time management techniques
- Find time to plan ahead, prioritise work and review it regularly
- Develop additional skills to increase your competence
- Build good relationships with colleagues
- Don't take work home or work late regularly
- Delegate work to the appropriate people
- Raise and discuss problems of communication with colleagues
- Work near a window and not in isolation, rearrange your work space and keep your desk tidy
- Take small, regular, healthy meals and take exercise at lunch time
- Find time to sleep, exercise, relax and have interests away from the job
- Find a balance between the job, family, friends, hobbies and other interests
- Relax regularly with a comedy television or radio programme
- Organise regular holidays as part of work planning and stick to the dates
- Consider a change of job and try to get one close to your hobby

8.6 Grievance, Disciplinary and Dismissal

Follow grievance, disciplinary and dismissal procedures carefully to avoid problems with other staff and to avoid litigation. In the first instance avoid problems through good management, but don't allow unacceptable behaviour to undermine your authority, affect other staff, lose customers or do other damage to the IT organisation.

Grievances

Grievances may be caused by external factors such as the workplace or distress caused by conflicts:

- Make the organisation's grievance procedures available to all staff
- Implement the procedures carefully
- Deal with grievances without delay to avoid further problems
- Get help if you are unfamiliar with the procedures
- Ensure that the supervisor has been consulted in the first place
- Arrange a mutually convenient time to meet with the member of staff
- Use an independent chairperson
- Bring in an observer such as the supervisor and invite the staff member to have a representative
- Assemble the facts, don't be biased and investigate the reasons
- Take notes for the staff file during the interview and give a typed copy to the member of staff
- Allow an appeals procedure to go to higher management/trade union

Disciplinary procedures

When a member of staff behaves in an unacceptable way and the situation requires a formal disciplinary process for reasons such as gross misconduct, consistently poor performance or unwarranted poor attendance:

- Make the organisation's disciplinary procedures available to all staff
- Implement the procedures carefully
- Get help if you are unfamiliar with the procedures
- Arrange a mutually convenient time to meet with the member of staff
- Use an independent chairperson
- Bring in an observer and invite the staff member to have a representative
- Assemble the facts, bring witnesses if serious, and don't be biased
- Take notes for the staff file during the interview and give a typed copy to the member of staff
- Allow an appeals procedure to go to higher management/trade union

Disciplinary penalties

The formal procedures need to be carried out on each occasion including for gross misconduct. It is usual to escalate disciplinary penalties (unless gross misconduct has occurred) and possible outcomes of hearings may be:

- An verbal warning
- Formal written warning
- Final written warning
- Suspension with or without pay during the investigation
- Transfer to another part of the organisation
- Dismissal with notice or pay in lieu of notice
- Instant dismissal for gross misconduct (such as drunkenness, fraud, stealing, assault)

Dismissal

If it is decided to dismiss a member of staff, involve the personnel section:

- Follow the organisation's procedures carefully and be sure of your grounds
- Get help if you are unfamiliar with the procedures
- Bring in an observer such as personnel and rehearse the procedures
- Be sure of the reasons (eg consistently poor performance, gross misconduct) and be fair
- Carry out the dismissal verbally and in writing
- Agree on an early date to leave, preferable immediately with pay in lieu of notice
- Keep the person under supervision, and get them out of the building instantly in the case of gross misconduct
- Keep staff informed, but observe any confidentialities

8.7 Staff Development

Staff development can take many forms, the main ones being working with others, learning from experience, studying and formal training. Over time use appropriate combinations of ways of developing staff.

Staff development

There are benefits both to the IT organisation and to individuals in improving their skills and ways to improve include:

- Allow staff opportunities to train others
- Allow staff to attend relevant seminars
- Allow staff to participate in special projects
- Consider allowing college study for relevant subjects
- Consider computer-assisted learning
- Consider following the standards for Investors In People
- Consider secondment to other areas
- Delegate work to staff who need the experience and are capable
- Enable covering for colleagues
- Enable job swapping and rotation of jobs
- Enable participation in formal meetings
- Enable some risk-taking in a managed situation
- Enable the study of other businesses
- Enable working in a group of staff with mixed skills
- Encourage staff to assess their own progress through informal reviews
- Give constructive feedback on mistakes
- Involve staff in the recruitment process
- Involve staff in think tanks and working groups
- Make reading material relevant to the job available
- Obtain feedback on staff from customers and management
- Organise informal group discussions
- Provide best practice models of work
- Provide experience on the job
- Provide formal training at the appropriate time
- Provide personal coaching or mentoring
- Within reason allow staff to train for their own career development, not just the organisation

8.8 Staff Training

Formal training of staff needs to be on-going where appropriate to the job, at the correct level, following analysis and discussion of needs with those involved, and where staff can immediately make use of it.

Most of the subjects in this handbook are potential areas for training, but the needs of the IT organisation must also be considered. Draw up a training plan addressing those needs, get it agreed with staff and management, implement it and record the action taken and results.

In some areas the training can be organised internally using suitably experienced staff, which will give those staff opportunities. In other cases external training will need to be brought in and a budget identified. Either way sit in on some of the training to assess its quality.

Training plan production

When drawing up a staff training plan:

- Document the business objectives leading to the training needs
- List the training areas required
- Allocate training in small doses rather than too concentrated
- Identify the staff to be trained (and give fair opportunities)
- Set target dates for training
- Produce a detailed specification of the training required
- Identify potential suppliers of the training and costs
- Consider tailored training if courses are not available
- Check out the previous experience of the potential suppliers
- Identify the best training facilities, preferably off the IT site
- Estimate the external and internal days and costs and identify the budget
- Negotiate and agree the needs with management
- Agree the needs with the staff to be trained
- Schedule the training to be 'just in time' so that work is immediately available

Training potential areas

Specifically, training or workshops may be useful in the following areas within the IT organisation:

- Business and systems analysis
- Fourth Generation Language development
- Windows NT, Internet, HTML, Java, Unix, Oracle
- Relational databases and their management
- Management reporting tools
- Networks and their management
- The PC office suite adopted as a standard for the organisation

Training documentation

Maintain the following documentation for training given:

- Training specifications (objectives, subjects covered, pre-requisites, duration)
- Training notification to staff form
- Training feedback from staff form (and obtain verbal feedback)
- Training history matrix for each member of staff (or hold it as part of a skills database)

8.9 Staff Appraisals

Staff performance appraisals will help individuals to improve their effectiveness, and will identify training and development needs, and thus ensure that the IT organisation has a skills resource. The appraisal should demonstrate the value of work done well, identify and build on strengths, and identify and address areas of weakness. It should also identify training needs, address any relationship problems, and provide planning information.

When addressing weak areas, identify two or three to be tackled, set goals, seek opportunities to enable staff to gain experience in these areas, and monitor progress regularly.

Organise the appropriate line managers to carry out regular appraisals of job performance, perhaps a formal one annually or biannually with progress reviews quarterly. To be effective the appraisal process must be objective and acceptable to all parties.

Ideally appraisal should not be linked to pay, but sometimes it is inevitable that a similar process has to be gone through for pay purposes, and a way of combining the two needs to be found.

Where the appraisal is not to be a formal one, hold a review with the person, with the emphasis on joint evaluation of progress, problems and targets for the future.

Appraisal outline

The following summarises a possible scenario for staff appraisal:

- Determine the appraisal timetable well ahead allowing sufficient time for appraisal/discussion
- Organise the line managers or supervisors to carry out the appraisal
- Agree over what period the appraisal is to be carried out (such as six months)
- Agree the competences required for each job (see the person specification) and their levels
- Competence levels must be objective and measurable for each skill
- Agree two or three non-routine key tasks for each member of staff based on these competences
- Agree with the individual how achievement of these tasks will be measured
- Identify opportunities to achieve these targets with each individual
- Identify possible barriers and what can be done about them
- At the end of the period collect evidence of achievement for each member of staff
- Obtain written self-appraisals from individuals on progress against the key tasks
- Organise line managers to interview each member of their team about the key tasks
- At the interview also consider the staff strengths, weaknesses, opportunities needed
- Obtain written line managers' appraisals of their staff and reconcile differences
- Standardise appraisals across groups to minimise misjudgements
- Document the results and their effectiveness for each individual
- Set new targets (don't set too many) based on weak areas for each person
- Document the proposed action including any training required
- Demonstrate evidence for any enhancement for individuals if the appraisal is linked to pay
- Summarise the results for management purposes
- Keep a matrix of staff competences to assist in the allocation of work

Competences: general

The measurement of general competences (skills plus experience) may be relevant in some situations and these include:

- Analysing
- Planning
- Organising
- Managing
- Decision making
- Communicating
- Social skills

Competences: specific

Detailed competences for IT staff should be those in the person specifications, linked to the job descriptions. Some potential competences (which could also be used in a skills database) include:

- Accountancy
- Budget management
- Business analysis
- Change management
- Contracting
- Customer care
- Database management
- Decision making
- Documentation production
- Estimating
- Internet/intranet development
- Management reporting
- Marketing
- Meetings management
- Negotiating
- Network skills
- Package evaluation
- Presentations
- Programming in various languages
- Project management
- Recruitment
- Report production
- Spread-sheets
- Staff appraisal
- Staff development
- Standards setting and monitoring
- System design and development
- Systems analysis
- Team management
- Technical expertise
- Tendering
- Training
- Work management
- Unix

Competence scales

Develop a few objective levels of competence which are specific, measurable and achievable when setting out criteria, possibly to assist with fixing pay scales, with levels such as:

Competence level achieved	Level code
No knowledge of the competence	0
A general knowledge through reading or training, but no practical experience	1
A small amount of practical experience through one or two projects	2
Considerable experience through several projects over at least two years	3
Considered to be an expert in the field and has trained others	4

Underachievement management

Where there are problems with underachievement deal with it in a positive but firm way to avoid the IT organisation being affected:

- Praise staff where warranted and thank them for work completed to a good standard
- Make any underachievement position clear to the person, but offer help
- Concentrate on measurable issues rather then emotional ones
- Identify the causes of the problems, but don't allow staff to bluff
- Possible causes include poor management such as imposed systems
- Consider training, coaching, job redesign
- Tackle lazy staff by setting mutually agreed deadlines on a weekly basis, daily if necessary

8.10 Managers' Competences

Managers' competences can be based on (i) having the knowledge (knowing what through training and experience), (ii) having the skill (knowing how), and (iii) having the right attitude and understanding (knowing why).

Managers' competences

Managers need to:

- Apply systems thinking and analysis to problems
- Be able and competent to manage change
- Behave commercially
- Exercise general management skills
- Know how to apply information technology to the business
- Know how to exploit business information and opportunities
- Manage finance
- Manage human resources
- Manage operations
- Be a team player
- Manage relationships well

Behaving commercially

To act in a business-like way:

- Understand commercial business practices
- Work towards achieving the objectives of the IT organisation
- Focus on customers and the services they want
- Understand customers' businesses and the services they themselves supply
- Understand the IT business context within customer organisations
- Be profit and cash conscious and supply quality products and services
- Understand the competition in the relevant commercial sector
- Understand and keep up to date on electronic commerce

Giving orders

When giving orders to employees:

- Ensure staff and their support structures are in place
- Use methodical and practical approaches to obtaining work from staff
- Consult with staff before giving orders and give them the reasons
- Set out clear goals to staff
- Don't necessarily over-praise staff
- Give instructions personally and back them up in writing
- Ensure staff understand the requirements of tasks set
- Ensure staff have the tools to carry out the job
- Think through outline plans for projects and staff beforehand
- Don't make unrealistic suggestions to staff as solutions to problems
- If you cannot think on your feet prepare better for meetings with staff

8.11 Appraisal of Managers

The appraisal of managers' can be carried out by the measurement of achievement within four groups of competences: (i) managing a quality service, (ii) managing resources, (iii) managing staff and (iv) managing oneself.

Managing a quality service

To deliver a quality service:

- Employ the elements of the ISO9000 regime
- Continually review customer needs and awareness
- Monitor to ensure that operational production complies with specifications
- Make decisions based on objective criteria
- Be aware of the context in which the service is being managed
- Review and assess the services provided on a regular basis

Managing resources

When managing staff and financial resources to deliver an overall service plan:

- Evaluate and plan the service delivery required
- Analyse resources and funding to maximise the use of resources
- Prioritise activities and ensure service delivery at the agreed quality and time
- Control the budget and be accountable through reporting back

Managing staff

When managing staff:

- Motivate staff and review their roles, responsibilities and performance
- Communicate vision, business plans, objectives and standards
- Listen to and support staff
- Delegate responsibility where appropriate
- Encourage team building to utilise skills and experience in projects
- Assess and provide training and coaching to staff
- Create effective working relationships with all contacts

Managing self

To be an effective manager:

- Be clear about the role and responsibilities of the post
- Prioritise and manage your personal workload satisfactorily
- Carry out self development to enhance your performance

8.12 Upwards Appraisal

Get feedback of the perception of management by staff through regular surveys produced by an independent body.

The following are some of the objective ways to recognise management success:

Business planning

When carrying out business planning good managers will:

- Show goals and objectives in written business plans
- Assess and identify the resources required to achieve the business goals
- Assess the training and development required to achieve the goals
- Explain the broad aims and objectives of the organisation and plans to staff
- Communicate with employees on a regular basis

Training and development

In terms of training and development good managers will:

- Introduce new employees into the organisation effectively through induction training
- Organise the training and development needed for new employees to do their jobs
- Understand the benefits of training and development
- Where appropriate link training to externally recognised standards
- Review training and development needs against the business objectives regularly
- Give opportunities to staff to discuss training and development needs regularly
- Involve individuals in agreeing the objectives and outcomes of any training and development
- Ensure training actually takes place where the need is identified
- Review the effectiveness of any training undertaken

8.13 Recruitment of Staff

Involve suitable staff in the recruitment process to motivate them, give them experience and encourage them to share responsibility. Plan the recruitment process carefully, formulate and agree the job description and the person specification, carry out the interview processes and select the most appropriate candidate.

Recruitment process

Plan for recruitment along the following lines:

- Follow the organisation's recognised recruitment procedures
- To manage the recruitment process form a panel of two or three including the post's manager
- Agree the overall timetable with the panel
- Agree the job description (the tasks required of the job)
- Agree the person specification (the skills required to carry out the tasks)
- Agree the advertisement and propose suitably targeted publications
- Agree the job description, person specification and advertisement with Human Resources
- Number and record the applications forms sent out with the date
- Record the applications received with the date
- Shortlist the applications received
- Agree the interview dates and times
- Notify shortlisted persons
- Notify shortlist failures if necessary
- Agree the questions for the interview based on the essential skills for the job
- Agree and document model answers
- Book a suitable interview room
- Arrange any disabled persons' needs
- Carry out the interviews, notifying Reception to expect the candidates
- Make offers, request references, arrange medicals
- Negotiate informal offer acceptances by phone
- Obtain formal written offer acceptances
- Notify Human Resources
- Notify existing staff of the result
- Notify interview failures

Job description formulation

When drawing up a job description:

- Provide a coherent series of related tasks for the job
- Ensure that the main tasks and responsibilities are clear
- Enable various skills to be used and opportunities to occur
- Include responsibility for the outcome of work and meeting mutually agreed deadlines
- Allow motivation, a degree of flexibility and a degree of own decision-making
- Enable contributions to the organisation and the job
- Provide a challenge and visible long-term goals
- Provide opportunities for learning, career development and training

Job description outline

When drawing up the detailed job description:

- Use a standard format for the job description for the whole organisation
- Give the organisation name and its business
- Give the job title and reference, the department, the location of the job
- Describe the purpose of the job and its position in the organisation
- Give the main responsibilities of the job grouped into logical functions
- Indicate the salary range and any other benefits
- Give the manager or supervisor title
- List the titles of staff the post is responsible for
- List the main internal and external contacts

Person specification

Use the job description to derive the attributes of the person needed to carry out the job:

- Use a standard format for the person specification for the whole organisation
- Give the job title and reference
- List the essential and desirable education required for the job
- Devise the competences for the job from a standard list for all staff that is also used in appraisals
- List the essential and desirable competences required for the job and the method of assessment
- List the essential/desirable experience/qualifications required and method of assessment
- List any other requirements of the job (such as travelling) and method of assessment
- Don't ask for age, sex, religion, race, marital status or family details
- Include an Equal Opportunities statement
- Ask applicants to respond to the person specification under each heading in order, rather than to the job description

Advertising for staff

Produce a concise advertisement from the key points in the job description and person specification, targeting the audience required:

- Decide on the best medium to target the staff required
- Start with the organisation name
- Give the department and its business
- Give the job title and reference
- Describe the purpose of the job and its position in the organisation
- Describe the location of the job
- List the main responsibilities grouped into logical functions
- Indicate the salary range and any other benefits
- Describe the working environment
- List the essential/desirable education and skills required for the job
- List the essential/desirable experience/qualifications required for the job
- List any other job requirements (such as travelling)
- Provide an Equal Opportunities statement
- Give the methods of obtaining application forms, contact, phone, fax, email and web addresses
- Provide the deadline for applications

Shortlisting applicants

When shortlisting applications for a job:

- Receive applications (perhaps via Administration) and date and number them
- Enable all panel members to read all applications and come to their own conclusions
- Reject applications not meeting those essential requirements linked to the application form
- Convene the panel to decide how to reduce the rest to a manageable number (perhaps 10 per job)
- Consider the use of the desirable requirements if there are too many applications
- Reconsider the job description (and possibly the salary) if there are too few applications

Interview preparation

In preparing for interviewing the applicants:

- Agree the interview dates and times, allowing sufficient time for discussion and breaks
- Decide who will welcome and look after the candidates during the interview process
- Notify shortlisted candidates of the date, time, location, disabled access, a contact, the agenda
- Consider requesting photographs of candidates to be interviewed to assist with their identification
- Notify shortlist failures if necessary
- Agree questions for the interview based on essential skills and who will ask what
- Decide whether to include written questions or exercises
- Agree and document model answers
- Book a suitable interview room
- Arrange any disabled persons' needs
- Notify Reception to expect the candidates

Interviewing

During the process of interviewing applicants for a job:

- Put an 'Interviews: Do Not Disturb' notice on the door
- Consider the use of identity labels for the panel
- Offer a drink to waiting candidates to help them relax
- Bring the candidate from the waiting area using the allocated welcome panel member
- Introduce the candidate to the panel and put them at ease
- Explain the format of the interview
- Outline the structure of the IT organisation and any parent organisation
- Outline the objectives of the IT organisation and the type of work it does
- Explain the form of project groups and their work
- Review the job applied for and how that fits into the organisation
- Review the application form in date order, concentrating on the most recent activities
- Look for gaps in the dates and explore them
- Encourage the candidate to talk about past work and colleagues, why moving, why this job
- Ask open questions to enable further exploration with follow-up questions
- Find out what the candidate has researched about the organisation
- Ask the prepared questions, the easy ones first, and note the answers
- The person chairing the panel should ask the first question, but others should participate
- The whole panel should make brief notes of answers to questions, but warn the candidate
- Alternatively make the notes at the end of the interview to avoid distracting the candidate
- Ask any other questions about personal circumstances
- Decide whether to verify the candidate's qualifications
- Invite the candidate's questions
- Outline the procedure for successful candidates and the likely timescales
- Provide handouts about the organisation
- Explain the medical and Equal Opportunities procedures, references, probationary period
- Go over the salary range, pension, benefits, leave, working hours, flexitime
- Explore the availability of the candidate
- Outline any interview or relocation expense schemes
- Provide a tour of the IT organisation for external candidates

Post-interview processes

Following the completion of the interviews the panel needs to:

- Review notes on all of the candidates together (photographs will help to recall faces)
- Base decisions on the essential skills and the answers to questions used to explore them
- Consider the whole panel's views with the chairperson having a casting vote
- Use points scored to separate equal candidates, similar to competence scales in appraisals
- Select a preferred candidate and a standby
- Inform failed internal candidates first to minimise de-motivation
- Negotiate informal offer acceptances by phone
- Make formal offers in writing, request references, send a new starter pack, arrange medicals
- Obtain formal offer acceptances in writing
- Ask Human Resources to prepare a contract of employment
- Notify existing staff of the result
- Notify interview failures
- Update any recruitment statistics kept
- Prepare to receive the new employee: desk, equipment, induction course and work

8.14 Job Seeking

Treat the process of seeking a job and being interviewed as a business process and carry out each stage of selling yourself in a professional way.

Job seeking preparation

In preparing to look for a job analyse and document as follows:

- Consider looking for a job that is close to your hobby
- Be prepared for the process to be a fairly full-time job if you are to succeed
- Seek out contacts and present yourself to potential employers
- Maintain a detailed CV with personal details, education, training, employment, skills, interests
- Consider using a close friend to help you assess yourself and to help construct your detailed CV
- Identify, understand and document your skills, experience and achievements
- Record instances where you played a part in processes and projects and thus gained skills
- Identify the areas where you think there may be a future and one which you could enjoy
- In education include yearly grading for degrees, qualifications, dates, responsibilities
- In training include courses, dates, any qualifications gained
- For employment give job, employer, number of staff, manager's title, experience, leaving reason
- Identify skills and knowledge in terms of personal skills, communications, managing people, managing processes, problem solving, numerical, creative and practical
- List interests such as languages, keyboard skills, computers, driving, hobbies, sports, clubs, public service, public speaking, voluntary work

Job hunting

When looking for a job:

- Don't necessarily go for the big companies; you may improve your chances with smaller ones
- Consider applying to areas of low unemployment in terms of location and job
- Research via the Internet, newspapers, agencies, job fairs, trade publications, networking
- Go for several jobs together to give you as much choice as possible
- Spend as much time as possible each day and aim to contact several companies per week
- Contact possible referees to ask permission to use them and who may themselves give you contacts
- Send your CV with a covering letter summarising your strong skills and their relevance to the job
- Maintain records of your research and letters to companies
- Follow up speculative mailshots and job applications with a phone call to prompt an interview

Job follow-up call

If making a speculative follow-up call for a job:

- Make sure you have researched the company, eg via the Internet
- Announce yourself and the job and ask if it would be OK to talk (don't ask if not OK)
- Address the person by title and surname until invited to do otherwise
- Get attention, create interest, create a desire to know more, encourage action
- Find out about the job requirements if they are not already known
- Avoid discussing current or desired salary at this stage
- If there are no possible job openings ask for leads to other potential areas within the organisation
- Keep notes of the conversations on a company file

Job application completion

A good job application will make all the difference to getting shortlisted for a job:

- Produce a quality typed application since only the best will be considered
- Respond to the Person Specification if any rather than the Job Description
- Respond to each of the person specification requirements in their printed order
- Start with the requirement title and summarise the skill and experience required
- Describe how your skills and experience meet the skills required with examples
- Never just list your skills or training you have received since you need to be believed
- Type it out well and make it succinct and readable otherwise it will not be considered properly
- Ensure you have responded to the application fully by rereading the instructions and requirements
- Reread your application several times, putting yourself in the position of the interviewers
- Get someone else to proof-read your CV, application and covering letter
- Ask for referees to be contacted only if the interview is successful
- Check with the persons you are asking to be referees before quoting them
- Post the application at least three days before the deadline
- Only enclose a CV if invited to do so
- Don't just cross-reference answers to your CV or to other answers – respond to each requirement

Curriculum Vitae

When drawing up a CV to send with a covering letter and job application:

- Target the summary CV to the job being applied for
- Create by reference to the detailed CV kept in your job history file
- Give your name, address, telephone number at the top
- Consider a passport-sized photo, perhaps scanned in
- Start with a personal profile that promotes your talents in less than 100 words
- Put in a few emboldened sub-headings
- Make some use of bulleted lists, but illustrate how you attained your skills and experience
- Emphasise your achievements and problem-solving skills
- Classify yourself broadly to give better scope for obtaining different work
- Decide whether to use chronological or functional order
- List your education history, qualifications obtained and when
- Detail your work history and any professional qualifications obtained
- Give a training summary from a detailed record kept in your job history file
- List your top skills including languages and be prepared to support them
- List your hobbies, social interests, driving record and be prepared to support them
- Avoid mentioning your current or desired salary if possible
- Give two references (work related, personal; asking permission first)
- Keep the CV to one page if possible, two maximum, backed if possible, to avoid boring the reader
- Use common typefaces such as Times New Roman or Garamond at 11 point
- Use bold on headings only and don't use underline, italic, brackets or inverted commas
- Print laser-quality and send the original document, not a copy
- Get someone to proof-read it
- Post unstapled in an A4 envelope
- Keep your detailed CV up to date for the future

Interview preparation

Prepare thoroughly for an interview to ensure you give it your best shot:

- Research the business of the company you are applying to, so that you are familiar with them
- Make use of the Internet or use the library and find out their main products and services
- Phone the company secretary to obtain company literature
- Research the kind of work you are applying for and its ramifications
- Find a contact who already works in that area and get them to coach you
- Ascertain the main tasks and skills from the job description and the person specification
- Use these to pre-empt the questions and associated details, such as statistics which may arise
- Write down these questions and formulate answers that you can memorise
- Prepare two or three questions to ask that you think won't be covered (see below)
- If required prepare a presentation using a PC or overhead projector (see Managing Presentations in Chapter 3)
- Make sure you and your clothes are clean and presentable
- Dress conservatively for the position applied for (find out about any dress code)
- Don't drink for 24 hours before and don't smoke for an hour before the interview
- Don't eat onions or garlic for 24 hours and chew a peppermint on the way to the interview
- Remember that first impressions count strongly
- Prepare a map and directions and ensure you are clear about these and the travel involved
- If at all possible travel to the location the day before and check out the route
- Arrive early at the location to allow for travel hold-ups and register just before the time due
- If part of the interview is group work make contact with other members of the group

Interview questions preparation

As well as trying to forecast the questions you may be asked that are directly related to the job description and person specification, think about the possible questions that often arise about your ambitions and qualities and how you will respond, including:

- Why you want the job you have applied for
- What qualities you would bring to the job
- Why you want to leave your present job
- Your (positive) views on your present company
- Whether you work best on your own or as part of a group (both)
- Your best quality (such as dealing with people or technical skills)
- Your long-term ambitions

Interview questions to ask

Towards the end of the interview you may be asked if there are any questions you wish to ask and it is best to take up the offer.. Often many of the areas you will think of will be covered during the interview so that you need to have a few prepared in writing.

Pick up ideas from the section on 'effective organisations' in Chapter 2 and consider questions such as:

- Why is the job open?
- How many others are being interviewed for the job and for how many posts?
- Where is the job located and what travel is involved?
- What would the first assignment of the job be?
- What formal or informal training will be provided?
- How is job performance evaluated?
- What potential is there in the job for career progression?
- What is the company's growth history and what are its future predictions?

Interview kit

You may need to take to the interview:

- A briefcase
- Company file and directions
- Contact phone numbers
- Copies of your CV in case they are needed
- Writing materials
- Work examples portfolio in case they are requested
- Any presentation required with overheads and handouts
- Job-related questions in writing to ask

Interview management

Management of the actual interview is critical and many decisions are made in the first few minutes of the interview:

- Make sure your mobile phone is switched off
- Walk in slowly, deliberately, head erect
- Wait to be asked to be seated following introductions
- Give a polite, firm handshake and smile
- Note the correct names of the panel and their positions
- Don't smoke even if invited to, but accept a drink
- Look alert, don't fidget, don't look at your watch
- Smile, use good eye contact, don't fold your arms, keep an open attitude
- Address the panel by titles and surnames until invited to do otherwise
- Keep your head up and maintain reasonable eye contact without staring
- Be positive about your current and past employers
- Respond to questions initially to the person asking, but then include the other members of the panel
- Listen to the questions, understand them and prepare a response route before answering
- Relax, respond succinctly but fully and to the point, speak clearly and reasonably slowly
- Consider whether the question asked is one you have forecasted
- Raise the points about the company you have rehearsed, having waited to see if they are answered
- Try to be positive even if your knowledge of the subject is weak
- Avoid asking about salary, holidays, benefits, an early decision
- At the end of the interview smile, thank the panel, shake hands and exit neatly
- If the interview included group work, consider going for a coffee with the group afterwards

Job application/interview tips

Some useful points to get over in the job application and interview are:

- Interviewers will be looking for skills, personality, interest in the job
- Show that you are a willing worker and able to learn
- Show that you can be managed, that you are a team worker but are able to work on your own
- Illustrate good communication skills, confidence, motivation, drive, technical skills if confident
- Behave professionally

Job application rejection

If your job application gets rejected:

- Don't be put off by a rejection letter
- Get used to rejection and bounce back, since employers prefer jolly people
- Phone the chairperson of the panel to get feedback on why you didn't get the job: persist with this
- Analyse why you weren't chosen on this occasion
- Compare the questions asked with those you prepared and improve your methodology
- Understand the need to get re-interviewed and use various ways to find work
- Use temporary or contract work to continue to get experience that may lead to a job
- Resist sliding back and continue training

Job offer

When you are offered a job:

- Spend 24 hours considering the offer
- Check the credentials of the company through Companies House and the Internet
- Get confirmation of your salary, starting date and any bonus arrangements
- Get the offer in writing before handing in your notice
- Consider waiting until references have been cleared before handing in your notice
- Ensure that any starting date proposed does not breach your current legal obligations
- Put your acceptance and any verbal agreements over the phone in writing

Working your notice

When you are leaving a job:

- Hand your notice in only when you have a written offer of a new job
- Negotiate an early release if possible, even if unpaid
- Accept that this is an interesting time of change, clear up your workload and make the most of it
- Continue to network with colleagues and contacts for possible future use
- Stick to the office rules and avoid sickness since you may still need a good reference
- Accept that you will be left out of meetings and other decision-making processes
- Leave verbal details and a written report of your work for hand-over, and how to contact you
- Contact your new employer to see what preparation you can do such as background reading
- Don't disclose any secrets or damage systems of the present organisation
- Throw a final party inviting all colleagues and contacts

8.15 Managing Yourself

Managing yourself is about how to deal with appraisal, improving your competences, working effectively with others, developing the right image and assertiveness, and managing your life.

Appraising staff

When appraising staff is one of your duties:

- Improve your own appraisal skills by training, reading and discussion of standards
- Develop staff to enhance their value to the organisation
- Adopt an attitude of striving for continuous development
- Provide guidelines to staff for future appraisals
- Appraise regularly such as quarterly and allow sufficient time such as an hour
- Set an agreed date and time and stick to it
- Prepare for the meeting by going over all papers beforehand
- Ensure that the appraisal is constructive and positive
- Use objective goals, measure progress towards them and discuss reasons for any failure
- Give praise where genuinely earned, but be sure you mean it
- Give constructive criticism where necessary, but don't put people down
- Get the person talking and explore relevant areas using your experience to coach
- Suggest ways to improve performance such as prioritisation, following standards, delegation
- Praise and build on strengths, and focus on weak areas to work on for the next appraisal
- Get the employee to summarise the intended actions with timescales and to document these
- Work towards putting the results of the appraisal in writing, but be sure of the content

Appraising yourself

When you are being appraised yourself:

- Work with your manager to ensure the appraisal is constructive and a success
- Prepare well using the guidelines provided and the goals agreed at the last appraisal
- Think where you want to get to, where you are now and how you will achieve the goal
- Don't take the opportunity to moan about the job and the organisation; be positive
- Summarise evidence of progress against targets
- Explore any bland statements given to obtain the reasons for them without anyone losing face
- Suggest training that will help both you and the organisation
- Keep your own notes of the meeting to check on any issued by the manager

Developing yourself

To assist with your career development:

- Know where you are now, where you want to go and how to get there
- Start planning early in your career
- Keep abreast of the organisation's successes or otherwise
- Accept that a career change may sometimes be necessary and not a bad thing
- Be realistic about your ambitions, strengths and weaknesses
- Read recommended subjects, generally keep well informed, discuss with colleagues and contacts
- Develop the grapevine to keep up with changes, technical issues etc
- Learn from your own experience
- Observe how experienced colleagues handle issues
- Ask for and look for opportunities to expand your skills
- Attend meetings, conferences, training courses, workshops
- Volunteer to take minutes and do them efficiently and effectively
- Take advantage of training in new areas
- Get relevant qualifications
- Review ways described under 'marketing methods' in Chapter 3

High achievement attainment

Use the following management strategies to attain high achievement:

- Anticipate possible failures and have contingency plans
- Be able to sum up alternative solutions to problems and the preferred option and why
- Be loyal to the organisation
- Be prepared to discuss how tasks will be done
- Be prepared to make unpopular decisions
- Be prepared to take calculated risks, following risk assessment
- Concentrate on the organisation's central issues
- Convey clearly in writing what you want done by others and when
- Deal with failures, learn from them and get on with the next job
- Enlist supporters for battles and prepare them
- Ensure that your top priority jobs are dealt with first
- Get broad support for policies from influential people in the organisation
- Go to social functions
- Join a professional body and belong to useful clubs
- Monitor your own and staff performances and take corrective action
- Network with influential people including your senior managers
- Produce a project plan for longer tasks with milestones and deliverables
- Reconcile your own needs with those of the organisation
- Recruit the best staff who also work well in teams
- Regularly summarise progress on all issues to more senior managers
- Review your own and staff performance and correct shortcomings
- Set demanding but achievable targets
- Show enthusiasm for tasks and encourage others to do the same
- Show perseverance, determination, sideways thinking
- Strive for the next goal when the current one is under control
- Take opportunities to speak, train, coach, interview, do voluntary work
- Understand the organisation's finances, key tasks and politics
- Volunteer to take on other challenges
- Work for winners and use others you admire as role models

Image management

Examine your own image with a view to improving it:

- Analyse your own weaknesses, discuss with a close friend and take actions to improve them
- Be prepared to defend the organisation
- Build a strong team around you
- Develop a sense of humour, smile and thank people for actions they have taken
- Don't criticise colleagues or competitors, don't broadcast bad feelings
- Dress to suit the occasion since first impressions with customers are always important
- Ensure you contribute to the organisation fully and use opportunities to illustrate this
- Keep your desk tidy and generally present an organised image
- Present a positive image and not a negative one
- Review your presence and actions against people you respect and move in their direction
- Support junior members of the team
- Turn failures into a positive image by illustrating actions taken to avoid them in future
- Wear clean clothes and appear smart and polished

Assertiveness

Improve your confidence by being assertive without being aggressive:

- Decide that you have worthwhile views on issues concerning your job
- Develop good working relationships with people
- Develop your own confidence through training and experience
- Don't accept unwarranted instruction or criticism without consideration and response
- Learn how to be assertive without being aggressive or unpleasant
- Don't say 'sorry' unnecessarily
- Manage stressful situations through a logical approach and avoid feeling threatened
- Take opportunities to practise speaking in public

Working for others

When working for others:

- Agree achievable deadlines and meet them
- Agree any resources required and how you will obtain them
- Agree the time and budget required and monitor them on a regular basis
- Anticipate requirements through your knowledge of current and future issues
- Be loyal to your manager and provide support
- Be positive when responding to requests for work and let the customer decide
- Consult over critical issues that may seriously impact management
- Don't openly criticise your manager or colleagues or blame someone else
- Form a good relationship and work with your manager or other sponsor
- Help your manager carry out promises made and meet deadlines
- Keep management informed, especially of problems and proposed solutions
- Keep promises made to your customers, manager and staff
- Own your own problems rather than unnecessarily wasting your manager's time
- Provide regular feed back on project progress (but not too often)
- Recognise the achievements of others through informal acknowledgement
- Take an interest in your manager's home life and hobbies
- Take opportunities to assist and impress your manager, suggest solutions to problems
- Understand the standards of performance required and work to them
- Understand what is required of you in the job and tasks and the critical success factors
- When consulting your manager gather together a number of issues for efficiency

Time management

Improve you own efficiency by managing your time better:

- Analyse how your time is spent
- Avoid constant interruptions from visitors and phone calls
- Avoid getting involved in too much of the detail of other peoples' work
- Avoid unnecessary meetings, ensure the objectives are established and limit their time
- Avoid unnecessary travel through the use of modern communications
- Be clear about your work objectives and tasks, priorities and timescales
- Concentrate on important work, correspondence and phone calls
- Concentrate thoughts, meetings and phone calls on the main business
- Consider telephone and video conferencing, electronic mail, fax
- Deal with top priority items when at your best, probably in a morning
- Don't fill your diary, but leave daily and weekly periods free to deal with unplanned work
- Don't put off unpleasant tasks
- Don't take on too many tasks in a day, and don't do the easy ones first
- Encourage the use of non-proprietary networked electronic diaries such as on the Internet
- Gradually reduce the time spent on tasks as skills increase
- Identify time-consuming low priority tasks in everyday work and review them
- Keep electronic and paper filing up-to-date or dump it
- Keep recent drafts of important documents in a 'recycle' drawer to enable emergency retrieval
- List daily and weekly tasks at the start of those periods and plan them
- Minimise paper handling and throw away unnecessary paper
- Organise colleagues and staff and delegate tasks to them
- Question the reason for tasks and the method of handling them
- Read correspondence while travelling on public transport if possible
- Set goals and deadlines for tasks
- Spend most of the time on the essential parts of the job

Working hours management

Consider the following to limit your working hours:

- Avoid unnecessary lengthy meetings and put instructions or decisions in writing
- Avoid unnecessary travel by delegation or by other means of communication
- Discuss crises with management and agree on a course of action
- Ensure that you have social interests, not just television, including getting physical exercise
- If you cannot avoid a lengthy day, decide on the reasons and consider action to avoid it
- Keep management informed of your workload and leave intentions
- Manage your work to avoid bringing work home regularly, thus avoiding family problems
- Observe how others manage their own workloads and pressures
- Plan, agree and book your leave well in advance and allow for it when planning work
- Tackle your own shortcomings first then consider prioritisation, delegation and extra staff
- Take interesting holidays but not necessarily expensive ones
- Think about how to tackle excessive demands for your time and have a written work plan
- Think long-term and plan work ahead to avoid crises and mistakes; become more efficient

Business start-up

If you set yourself up in business:

- Consider partners with suitable qualities to share ideas, skills, costs, work
- Contact the DTI and Business Links (under Business Enterprise Agencies in Yellow Pages). for leaflets and advice
- Decide what kind of business: Limited, Private, Partnership
- Carry out market research to ensure that there is a demand
- Develop a personal business plan (see Business Planning in Chapter 2)
- Decide how you will protect your ideas
- Get free advice from friends with experience, bank managers, accountants, solicitors
- Seek out a recommended accountant for advice, book keeping, tax return, contracting
- Decide how you can best borrow capital without risking your home and family
- With your accountant decide if you need to register for VAT
- Register the name of the company with the Business Enterprise Agency
- Open a business bank account
- Take out business insurance, including public liability
- Take out a pension plan and insurance against illness
- Consider continuing with your present job initially
- Consider whether you can work from home until the business is established
- Decide which is the best way to advertise (see 'business plan' in Chapter 2)
- Set up a web site and email address with short mnemonics relevant to the business
- Create stationary for letters, orders, invoices etc
- Seek out an accounting package and register with Data Protection if necessary
- Ensure all costs are included when working out the cost of services and products (see 'business plan' in Chapter 2)
- Register as self-employed for National Insurance purposes, unless still employed elsewhere
- Budget over the year for tax payments and advance payments
- Keep materials to a minimum and buy 'just in time' but have alternative sources
- Keep and register all invoices and receipts for tax purposes
- Account for all bills rendered and their payment, chase debtors
- Ensure that you achieve both a profit and a good cash flow
- Offset all reasonable business expenses against income for tax purposes
- Be prepared to persevere for two years without profit
- Set personal goals each year, month, week, day
- Maintain contact with other people in associated businesses
- Separate work from leisure time
- Take regular holidays

8.16 Socialising

A skill which some find hard to acquire is the ability to mix and communicate with people successfully. Social skills are essential to make serious progress in almost any field and any difficulties must be overcome through practice and turned into positive enjoyment.

Socialising benefits

The benefits of socialising with people include:

- Your self-confidence will increase
- There will be increased comfort and enjoyment in the job
- You will be perceived as in control
- You will establish links with useful people
- You will increase your customers
- You will obtain new information and understanding
- There will be better career opportunities

Getting to know people

Expand your social circle:

- Attend social events and be prepared to talk to anyone
- Introduce yourself instead of waiting to be introduced
- Be able to talk about the current headlines, sport, travel, anything
- If rejected, move on to someone else
- Avoid sexual signals through dress, body language, touching, double meanings

Function attendance

When preparing to attend a function:

- Identify the benefits of the event such as an increased network of contacts
- If appropriate get a list of attendees in advance and memorise those people you want to meet
- Prepare small talk
- Practise a firm handshake for greeting, deals and departing
- Ensure handshakes for all, men and women
- Avoid kissing, especially on the mouth or in the office
- Ensure good eye contact and smile
- Don't let things get too serious
- Ensure business cards are up-to-date and available
- Collect business cards and add notes to help memorise people
- Only hand out expensive brochures to really interested customers

Social guidelines

The following guidelines will be useful for social events:

- Dress for the occasion
- Avoid smoking
- Don't eat or drink too much and drink plenty of water
- Don't put people down
- Don't monopolise one person
- Don't just talk to apparently important people
- Don't patronise particular groups of people
- Don't be too loud
- Don't complain and be positive
- Carry out promises made

9. ADMINISTRATION, FINANCE AND PROPERTY

Part of the job of a manager will be routine administration and management. This chapter deals with staff administration areas, managing Health & Safety, budget generation and monitoring, and property management.

9.1 Administration Procedures

Make written procedures available to staff to cover most administration areas as part of a standards and guidelines handbook.

Administration areas

Guidelines for staff are likely to be required in the following administration areas:

- Accident reporting procedures
- Appraisals procedures
- Attendance sheets
- Clock cards and time sheets
- Data Protection guidelines
- Disciplinary procedures
- Fire alarm procedures
- Grievance procedures
- Harassment procedures
- Health & Safety procedures
- Leave authorisation and recording
- Recruitment procedures
- Security standards
- Sickness procedures and monitoring
- Staff management arrangements
- Staff resource allocation
- Training arrangements

New employee induction

As part of the initial induction of a new employee:

- Go over the physical layout of the IT organisation
- Indicate fire escapes and fire alarm arrangements
- Review the new employee's skills, experience and qualifications
- Outline the structure and purpose of the whole organisation and its key employees
- Outline the structure and purpose of the IT organisation and its products and services
- Go over the key employees of the IT organisation
- Outline the IT customers and their needs and how the new employee will fit in
- Go over key rules, procedures, guidelines, internal politics
- Go over pay issues, method of payment, pension, probationary period, unions
- Outline arrangements for working hours, clock cards, time sheets, breaks, lunch, leave, sickness
- Outline the use of telephones, mail, electronic mail, fax
- Indicate the functions of the Administration group
- Outline Equal Opportunities and harassment issues
- Outline the procedures for problems, complaints, grievance, disciplinary issues
- Outline Data Protection responsibilities
- Introduce security standards including data security
- Go over system and user password security, including ways of devising secure passwords
- Outline Health & Safety issues including medical facilities and hazards
- Indicate potential training and development areas
- Outline any formal induction training planned
- List colleagues' names and their roles in the organisation
- Introduce the supervisor and colleagues and agree on a mentor
- Tour the organisation and introduce staff
- Provide background reading such as an IT organisation handbook
- Get feedback from the new employee on the success of the induction process

Time analysis

Reports on the use of human resources can be a by-product of the work management process and various ad-hoc analyses can be produced to assist with monitoring, especially if a project management or work management package has been used.

For business planning purposes, and at year end, it is useful to analyse time spent by activity and publish percentages of productive and non-productive time overall. Use this to illustrate the typical staff activity profile and to derive recharge rates for estimating purposes.

Analyse staff time in various ways using a management reporting tool:

- Use a work management, project management or time analysis database to produce ad-hoc reports
- Analyse work by project and by person to help monitor activities on a daily basis
- Analyse work for planning purposes by type of activity including non-productive time

Progress reports

Produce progress reports to management on a monthly basis in a form that is concise and informative, quantifying issues on each of the current projects:

- Produce progress reports on time since there is no advantage in being late
- Produce reports in the '3Ps' format (Progress, Problems, Plans) for each area of work
- Be concise and use bullet points where appropriate
- Only report issues relevant to management
- Quantify issues and be informative
- Report on staff and their progress against targets set

9.2 Health & Safety Regulations

Managers are responsible for Health & Safety issues in the workplace and staff need to be familiar with the Health & Safety Regulations. Managers and staff need to be trained to deal with all aspects of health and safety, including risk assessment of the work environment. Regular reviews of the workplace must be undertaken and the risks assessed and dealt with. The building, the equipment in the building and staff practices all need examination.

Health & Safety organisation

Health & Safety issues to be organised include:

- Arrange a procedure for reporting accidents
- Publish the location of first aid boxes
- Train volunteers in first aid and publish their names to staff
- Provide fire fighting equipment, detectors and alarms
- Arrange for fire alarms and equipment to be inspected at the correct intervals
- Ensure that the building has fire exits marked and has independent lighting
- Display fire alarm procedures and carry out regular tests and drills
- Train fire wardens to be familiar with the alarm system and procedures and ensure one is on duty
- Keep stairways and passages clear of waste
- Clearly mark hazardous areas and machinery
- Arrange regular eyesight checks for staff using computer screens

Office risk assessment

When assessing Health & Safety risks in the office cover the following issues:

- Ensure that sufficient space per employee has been allocated
- Ensure that lighting is adequate and is working correctly
- Monitor the temperature to ensure that it is within the permitted range
- Ensure that there is adequate ventilation and avoid fumes from copiers and printers
- Ensure that the noise level is acceptable
- Run cables under floors or in ceilings, not over the floor with covers
- Provide computer screens with reasonable clarity and brightness and without a flicker
- Site computer screens to avoid window or lighting reflections
- Provide adjustable, comfortable office chairs with five castors
- Ensure that office furniture is not dangerous
- Ensure that there isn't any waste paper or other waste materials lying around

Managers' Health & Safety role

Managers are responsible for Health & Safety issues in their own areas:

- Take management responsibilities for the Health & Safety of staff and public seriously
- Plan activities to prevent accidents in the workplace for which you are responsible
- Carry out Health & Safety checks every three months and action any issues found
- Arrange to record accidents, reporting life-threatening ones to the Health & Safety Executive
- Carry out further checks after accidents or serious incidents
- Provide training for staff on the rules, procedures, safe working, responsibilities
- Arrange for deputies to take over from managers in their absence
- Ensure that visitors and sub-contractors are familiar with fire alarm procedures
- Arrange for regular renewal of fire, electrical and gas safety certificates

Employees' Health & Safety role

Employees also have a role to play in Health & Safety:

- Be familiar with the person in charge of health & safety in your group
- Take reasonable care to ensure that you don't endanger yourself or others
- Co-operate with employers and staff to help meet the statutory requirements
- Don't interfere with or misuse things provided in the interests of health and safety
- Ensure that you are familiar with fire escapes, alarms, types of extinguisher and their use
- Report any hazards such as trailing cables, waste paper, locked fire escapes, dangerous storage
- Fill filing cabinets from the bottom and only open one drawer at a time
- Ensure fire doors are not propped open
- Know how to get first aid assistance

9.3 Budget Management

A number of controls and key indicators will need to be monitored to judge the success of the IT organisation, the most important of which will be the financial monitors.

Business controls

Decide which are the key controls and performance indicators for the IT organisation:

- Ensure that business controls are practical, measurable and not too numerous
- Use work management and charging systems to provide data for the controls
- Monitor the budget for all services, teams, customers, the IT organisation
- Monitor deadlines for projects and support arrangements
- Monitor the standard of services by quality audit checks and through feedback from customers
- Monitor customer care both within (including teams) and outside the IT organisation

Budget preparation

When competing for budgets:

- Decide on the appropriate approach to the activities for which budgets are sought
- Prepare accurate estimates under each expenditure heading for these activities
- Base the estimates on previous experience adjusted for likely variances
- To help sell the budget request record the details behind the estimate and the benefits
- Include the likely profile of expenditure and income over sub-periods such as months
- Review estimates with deputies and team leaders then accountants and management
- Record the results in a standard format to enable merging with other estimates and to allow monitoring

Budget cuts

Budget cuts may requested by the organisation's management board:

- Budget cuts are often a board decision to be complied with, but sometimes a first test
- Get to know the financial director or accountant in charge of suggesting areas for cutting
- Review existing costs to look for savings in anticipation of cuts
- Prepare and present the options, which will often be potential staff cuts
- Make out special cases rather than ignore the rulings
- Consider other options for the supply of labour, services, materials, accommodation
- Check leasing costs to ensure that they are yours and that they are correct
- Ensure that overheads such as accommodation and administration are allocated fairly
- Review methods of allocating costs and income to ensure a fair distribution
- Provide information to ensure that informed cuts take place
- Look for early signs that the IT organisation could be affected
- Reassure staff that their issues will be considered

Budget monitoring

When organising the processes for monitoring the IT organisation's budgets:

- Encourage the devolvement of budgets and their monitoring
- Use a computer system to hold the original estimates, and income and expenditure profiles
- Capture actual expenditure as a by-product of a work management system
- Capture income and payments from the associated customer charging system
- Compare actual budgets with estimates on a regular basis such as weekly
- Compare overall and at each budget heading such as a job and a customer
- Investigate reasons for variations, take corrective action, report exceptions
- Keep the team and management informed of the position in writing

Invoice payment

When paying invoices make sure that they have been coded to the correct budget heading and that the budget has been authorised:

- Separate out the ordering and invoice payment functions to different bodies
- Ensure orders have the correct analysis code attached to reflect the budget heading
- Check invoices back to the contract and the authority to spend

9.4 Property Management

When inspecting buildings intended for new offices or domestic accommodation, examine and record physical details of the property and its supplies, and estimate running costs. Take along the appropriate tools to carry out the inspection and be prepared to get into roof spaces and under floors.

Property tool kit

Include the following tools when inspecting properties:

- Check list, pad, pen, tape measure
- A short ladder (4 metres)
- Binoculars to see the roof
- Torch
- Possibly a camera
- Electrical screwdriver to see wiring
- Knife to check woodwork
- Possibly a damp meter

Property general details

Record the general property details:

- Property address
- Owner/agent, address, contact, phone number
- Date property inspected
- General description of the property
- Summary of the accommodation provided
- Outbuildings
- Geographical orientation
- Age of the property
- Summary of construction
- Insurance risks
- Council rates or tax band
- Freehold/leasehold
- Ground rent/chief rent and holder
- Any existing tenancies
- Details of access to the property
- Disabled access and facilities
- Details of conservation areas, buildings
- Parking facilities
- Roads, footpaths, rights of way
- Gardens
- Public transport availability
- Motorway access
- Location and amenities
- Future development in the area
- Noise in the vicinity
- Crime in the area
- Security against burglars and vandals

Property mains supplies

Check on the main supplies for:

- Water, including drinking, age of pipes
- Electricity and electrical inspection certificate, distribution board, age
- Gas and gas inspection certificate
- Sewerage including inspection covers
- Telephones
- Networking

Property external condition

Inspect and record the external condition of the building:

- Roofs
- Gutters and spouts
- Chimney stacks and flues
- Main walls and pointing
- Gable ends and bay windows (look for bulges)
- Damp courses
- Drains/drainage
- Joinery including windows and doors
- External decoration
- Outbuildings
- Site/gardens/fencing
- Trees and any preservation orders

Property rooms

Record the building's rooms, including sizes, under headings such as:

- Basement/cellars
- Bedrooms
- Box room/storage
- Cloak room
- Dining area
- Kitchen
- Living room
- Offices
- Roof space
- Stairs/lift

Property internal condition

Inspect and record the internal condition of the building for each room for:

- Air conditioning
- Ceilings
- Central heating
- Computer/phone network
- Curtain rails/blinds
- Dampness
- Decoration
- Fireplaces, flues and chimneys
- Floor covering
- Floors
- Gas
- Heating
- Hot water
- Insulation
- Joinery
- Kitchen fittings
- Lighting
- Phone points
- Plumbing
- Power points (including sufficiency)
- Sanitary ware
- Service boards
- Television points
- Thermostats
- Ventilation
- Walls and partitions
- Water
- Wiring
- Woodworm and dry rot

Building finance

When working out the cost of running a property don't forget:

- Building insurance
- Commercial Rates or Council Tax
- Contents insurance
- Electricity
- Gas
- Ground rent/chief rent
- Leasing costs
- Mortgage repayments
- Repairs
- Service costs
- Telephones
- Water rates

Property summary

Summarise initial conclusions about the property:

- Asking price or rent
- Considered value
- The cost of essential work
- The running costs
- Any special problems
- Outlook
- Positive points
- Negative points
- Negotiation areas
- Overall impression

9.5 Building Alteration Costs

When considering alterations to buildings get estimates, agree the form of contract and ensure that all elements of building costs are identified to avoid unpleasant surprises. For longer jobs use a contract, make stage payments as targets are reached, but retain 10% until satisfied with the job.

Building estimates/contracts

When getting estimates and contracting for building work:

- Use recommended firms, preferably members of a trade association
- Write down a schedule of what wants doing
- Get three written quotations
- Ensure all elements of building work are included
- Don't forget VAT
- For longer jobs use a contract such as the JCT Minor Works Contract
- Make stage payments and agree to retain 10% to ensure problems get sorted
- Don't pay up front except to purchase expensive materials
- Monitor the job on a daily basis

Building planning

When estimating the costs of changes to a building consider:

- The planning permission process
- Listed building/conservation issues
- Building Regulations approval
- Surveyor costs
- Architect costs
- Structural Engineer costs
- Solicitor costs

Building labour

When considering alterations or repairs to a property don't forget the labour costs of:

- Project management
- Building
- Carpentry
- Electrical
- Plumbing
- Plastering
- Tiling
- Decorating
- Interior designing
- Computer/phone networking
- Carpets/flooring

Building materials

When considering alterations or repairs to a property don't forget the material costs of:

- Building
- Carpets/flooring
- Computers and phones
- Damp proofing and rot treatment
- Decorating
- Double glazing
- Electrical/lighting
- Joinery
- Kitchen
- Networking
- Office furniture
- Plastering
- Structural
- Tiling and grouting
- Washrooms/toilets/bathroom

10. NATIONAL MANAGEMENT STANDARDS

The UK National Management Standards were developed by the Management Charter Initiative and are Crown Copyright. They are used as the basis for the NVQ management teaching syllabus and for information the unit letters are shown in the summary. All of the activities except Managing Energy are relevant to the management of IT and have been covered in this handbook.

Experience in almost all of these activities is achievable even if only at a modest level. The list can be used to check off experience or the lack of it and thereby take some corrective action by looking for and asking for opportunities.

Crown Copyright is reproduced with the permission of the Controller of Her Majesty's Stationery Office.

A. Managing Activities

Manage the operation to meet customers' requirements, to improve work activities, to manage change and operating environments and to establish strategies and evaluate organisational performance:

- Maintain work activities to meet requirements
- Maintain healthy, safe and productive working conditions
- Make recommendations for improvements to work activities
- Implement plans to meet customers' requirements
- Maintain a healthy, safe and productive work environment
- Ensure products and services meet quality requirements
- Agree customer requirements
- Plan activities to meet customer requirements
- Ensure products and services meet customer requirements
- Improve work activities
- Recommend improvements to organisational plans
- Identify opportunities for improvements in activities
- Evaluate proposed changes for benefits and disadvantages
- Plan the implementation of change in activities
- Agree the introduction of change
- Implement changes in activities
- Analyse the organisation's external operating environment
- Evaluate competitors and collaborators
- Develop effective relationships with stakeholders
- Review the organisation's structures and systems
- Create a shared vision and mission to give purpose to the organisation
- Define values and policies to guide the work of the organisation
- Formulate objectives and strategies to guide the organisation
- Gain support for organisational strategies
- Develop measures and criteria to evaluate the organisation's performance
- Evaluate the organisation's performance
- Explain the causes of success and failure in organisational strategies

B. Managing Resources

Plan and use non-human resources efficiently, determine their effectiveness and secure financial resources for plans:

- Make recommendations for the use of resources
- Contribute to the control of resources
- Plan the use of physical resources
- Obtain physical resources
- Ensure the availability of supplies
- Monitor the use of physical resources
- Make recommendations for expenditure
- Make proposals for expenditure on programmes of work
- Agree budgets for programmes of work
- Control expenditure and activities against budgets
- Review the generation and allocation of financial resources
- Evaluate proposals for expenditure
- Obtain financial resources for the organisation's activities

C. Managing People

Develop and manage yourself and staff resources, develop productive relationships, and select staff for tasks:

- Develop your own skills to improve your performance
- Manage your time to meet your objectives
- Develop yourself to improve your performance
- Manage your own time and resources to meet your objectives
- Continuously develop your own knowledge and skills
- Optimise your own resources to meet your objectives
- Gain the trust and support of colleagues and team members
- Gain the trust and support of your manager
- Minimise conflict in your team
- Develop the trust and support of colleagues and team members
- Develop the trust and support of your manager
- Minimise interpersonal conflict
- Enhance the trust and support of colleagues
- Enhance the trust and support of those to whom you report
- Provide guidance on values at work
- Contribute to identifying personnel requirements
- Contribute to selecting required personnel
- Identify personnel requirements
- Select required personnel
- Contribute to the identification of development needs
- Contribute to planning the development of teams and individuals
- Contribute to development activities
- Contribute to the assessment of people against development activities
- Identify the development needs of teams and individuals
- Plan the development of teams and individuals
- Develop teams to improve performance
- Support individual learning and development
- Assess the development of teams and individuals
- Improve the development of teams and individuals
- Assess the effectiveness of management teams
- Improve the effectiveness of management teams
- Plan the work of teams and individuals
- Assess the work of teams and individuals
- Provide feedback to teams and individuals on their work
- Allocate work to teams and individuals
- Agree objectives and work plans with teams and individuals
- Assess the performance of teams and individuals
- Provide feedback to teams and individuals on their performance
- Delegate responsibility and authority to others
- Agree targets for delegated work
- Provide advice and support for delegated work
- Promote and protect delegated work and those who carry it out
- Help team members who have problems affecting their performance
- Contribute to implementing disciplinary and grievance procedures
- Support team members who have problems affecting their performance
- Implement disciplinary and grievance procedures
- Dismiss team members whose performance is unsatisfactory
- Plan the redeployment of personnel
- Redeploy personnel
- Make personnel redundant

D. Managing Information

Lead and contribute to meetings, and obtain, analyse and use information effectively:

- Gather required information
- Inform and advise others
- Hold meetings
- Lead meetings
- Make contributions to meetings
- Chair meetings
- Participate in meetings
- Obtain information for decision making
- Record and store information
- Analyse information to support decision making
- Advise and inform others
- Identify information and communication requirements
- Select information management and communication systems
- Implement information management and communication systems
- Monitor information management and communication systems
- Obtain information needed to take critical decisions
- Analyse information for decision-making
- Take critical decisions
- Advise and inform others

E. Managing Energy

Managing energy is outside the scope of this handbook, but the checklist of management standards is included here for completeness. These general processes could be applied to other management areas.

- Audit the organisation's performance in the way it manages energy
- Identify improvements to the way the organisation manages energy
- Provide advice on the development of policies for the use of energy
- Recommend strategies to implement energy policies
- Promote energy efficiency throughout the organisation
- Promote the organisation's achievements in energy efficiency
- Establish systems and processes to monitor and evaluate usage
- Obtain, analyse and record information on energy efficiency performance
- Evaluate the organisation's energy efficiency performance
- Identify opportunities to improve energy efficiency
- Recommend improvements to energy efficiency
- Support the development of a culture of energy awareness
- Provide advice and support for energy efficient practices
- Provide support for the development of systems to measure energy use
- Provide support for the collection, analysis and recording of information on energy usage
- Provide advice on trends and developments in energy usage
- Encourage involvement in energy efficiency activities
- Provide advice on the competences needed to use energy efficiently
- Provide advice on the training needed to use energy efficiently
- Establish the organisation's position in the marketplace
- Identify market changes likely to affect supplies
- Determine the competitiveness of supplies from the market
- Identify beneficial developments relating to supplies and sources

F. Managing Quality

Promote the idea of total quality management as part of the organisation's strategy to produce quality products and services:

- Promote the importance of quality in the organisation's strategy
- Promote quality throughout the organisation and its customer and supplier networks
- Provide advice and support for the development of quality policies
- Provide advice and support for the development of strategies to implement quality policies
- Develop and implement systems to monitor and evaluate organisational performance
- Promote continuous quality improvements for products, services and processes
- Establish quality assurance systems
- Maintain quality assurance systems
- Recommend improvements to quality assurance systems
- Provide advice and support for the assessment of processes and working environments
- Provide advice and support for the development of plans to improve quality systems
- Provide advice and support for the development of quality measurement systems
- Provide advice and support for the collection, analysis and documentation of information
- Plan to audit compliance with quality systems
- Implement the quality audit plan
- Report on compliance with quality systems
- Audit compliance with quality systems
- Follow up quality audits

G. Managing Projects

Formally plan and control all of the main activities of the organisation:

- Clarify the project's scope and definition
- Provide plans to achieve the project's goals
- Contribute to project preparation
- Support the project team
- Co-ordinate activities, resources and plans
- Keep stakeholders informed of project progress
- Complete project activities
- Contribute to the evaluation of project planning and implementation
- Agree the project's scope and definition with the sponsor
- Develop plans to achieve the project's goals
- Establish the project's resourcing and control methods
- Lead the project team
- Monitor and adjust activities, resources and plans
- Develop solutions to project problems
- Maintain communication with project stakeholders
- Ensure the completion of project activities
- Evaluate the effectiveness of the project planning and implementation

11. ACCOUNTING TERMS

This section defines some of the accounting terms that IT staff are likely to encounter when they are discussing costing and financial management systems with customers.

Accountancy codes
Income and expenditure codes are used to enable analyses of charges and costs to be made over budget headings and hence to monitor income and costs. Both types of these revenue accountancy codes are usually structured into objective (building, departmental unit, person, vehicle or anything else one needs to control costs on) and subjective (the type of income or cost such as type of work done, the budget heading).

Accounting period
Accountants work to an accounting year and week (which may not be the same as the tax year and week). The year will normally be broken down into calendar months of four or five weeks. The accountant will want to be able to produce a trial trading account and a cash flow statement for at least each month. The trading account will show any profit or loss and involves income and costs. The cash flow statement looks at payments going out for payroll and purchase invoices, and at payments coming in from sales invoices, and at stock balances. Within the accounting period the accountant needs to know about purchase orders, goods received, purchase invoices paid, payroll costs, sales invoiced, sales paid, areas of sales, and stock held. This will enable a view of the state of the accounts and forecast problems such as making a profit on paper but not having enough cash flow to pay the bills.

Accruals
Accruals are monies committed through obligations incurred to pay bills but before the goods are received; confusingly often referred to as commitments. Accruals are normally more important than commitments to businesses.

Actual costs
Actual costs are calculated from the actual time taken to do work, taken from timesheets or job cards and posted against estimates for budget monitoring purposes. A job could consist of mixed standard schedule-of-rates and dayworks, in which case the actual time would have been split between the two types of work (or booked back to each schedule (work item, task)). For schedule-of-rates tasks the actual would be used to see if a profit had been made; for dayworks the actual time would also be the charge. Actual costs are not usually booked back against every task if these are small and sometimes a first work item with a dummy schedule on it with no charge is used to collect costs.

Balance sheet
The balance sheet describes the overall financial position of the business at a moment in time. It shows the assets in use (premises, cash etc) and the sources of finance being used to acquire those assets (such as capital, loans and creditors).

Budgets
Rather than allow unlimited expenditure on a budget heading such as new IT development for a particular project, it is usual to agree a planned allocation of resources. Similarly budgets must be set for any project in order to ensure that job can be paid for. Budgets may not be straight line over a period but may be profiled and will be monitored over time against actual expenditure or income.

Budget heading
The subjective part of an income or expenditure code, which relates to the type of income/expenditure.

Cash flow statement
A cash flow statement consists of the following accounts for a period: opening balance, plus income, less expenditure (all payroll costs, overheads, finance charges, storage) to form a net carried forward balance.

Commitments
Commitments are monies committed through the placing of orders, having received the goods but not paid the invoices. Commitments are important to budget-based services.

Contra accounts
Any automatic or manual entry into the general ledger will have an equal and opposite summary entry, thus ensuring a net balance of zero transactions. (Revenue accounts often start afresh each financial year but capital accounts have brought forward balances.) The contras can be used to form control accounts which feed into the production of the final accounts. An example would be: deductions for Income Tax in payroll would be contra to an account; when the monthly payment is made to the Inland Revenue a further contra goes next to the original (and would be equal and opposite to it if done in the same period).

Control totals
All financial systems need a short (daily or weekly) accounting period for which time it is possible to analyse monies by type of transaction. The reasons for this include providing a means of manually ensuring that a system passes on the correct total to another system, providing a means of breaking down a process to find an error, and providing a statistical analysis. Thus it is usual to provide, for example, an analysis of a weekly batch process by type of transaction, showing the brought forward cumulative totals, changes this week and carried forward. In addition it is usual to hold the brought forward figures on a file and automatically check that they are correct against the detailed records from the cumulative file. Further, in case there are problems reconciling figures, it is usual to provide the control totals at a lower level so that a manual inspection could be made to find an error.

Cost plus
A way of referring to dayworks.

Cost centre
A cost centre is a unit to which budgets are allocated and which is controlled by a cost centre manager. Actual costs incurred are directed to a cost centre, monitored against the budget and formally reported. The cost centre may be a building, vehicle, person or a group of any of these, that is an object, and the cost centre is the objective part of an accountancy code. A cost centre could cover part of a building, a whole building, or several buildings widely separated. A cost centre manager will typically control several budget headings. The budget heading is the type of work being done and equates to the subjective part of an accountancy code.

Costing system
The general term for any system that records costs (and usually charges), which enables intermediate and final accounts to be produced, assists with operational controls, enables the cost of products to be derived for pricing purposes and enables profitable areas to be identified by comparison with standard costs.Costs and charges. From the point of view of the contractor charges are the price of the jobs being carried out and invoiced to customers and become the contractor's income (whether or not it is paid). The contractor's costs are payroll and materials costs and overheads. The difference between the contractor's costs and charges is the profit or loss. The contractor's charges become the customer's costs. A contractor's IT system will often hold both cost and charge rates. These may be the same, but hourly costs may vary with labour agreements whereas charge rates will probably be fixed for a contract.

Accounting Terms

Dayworks
This method of charging is where the agreement with the customer is that the labour charge will be on an hourly or daily basis. This would often be linked to supplying the materials at cost price plus a handling charge.

Double entry accounting
The principal is that two entries are always made for any transaction recorded, one a debit entry and one a credit. The second entry can then be used as a control (summary) account. For example all purchases are first recorded in a purchase ledger but need to go to the general ledger to form part of the final accounts. Similarly income would be recorded in a sales ledger (which also deals with the actual recovery of monies owed) and passed to the general ledger. Income would be entered as a summary analysis (not usually for each job) and for every income entry into the general ledger there would be an equal and opposite entry to a balancing account. Similarly expenditure entries (payroll, purchases) would have contra accounts, making the net entry zero.

Factoring
Factoring is the sale of debts to an outside agency specialising in debt collection for the purposes of improving the cash flow of the organisation.

Financial Accounting
Financial accounting is primarily concerned with looking backwards and reporting on the state of finances. This involves the recording of daily financial transactions such as sales, purchases, payments and receipts. From these records three main documents are produced: (i) the profit/loss statement, (ii) the balance sheet and (iii) the cash flow statement. To enable monitoring of the financial state of the organisation to take place estimates of expenditure and income will be produced annually, broken down into periods such as months or weeks. Business transaction costs, charges, payments and receipts will be recorded to enable the final accounts of the organisation to be produced and to enable monitoring against period profiles to take place.

Internal Trading Units
Internal trading unit accounting is a mechanism for sub-contracting a job into several others. The highest level job would produce the charge to the customer but costs would be fed back to the lowest level jobs whose charges themselves become costs to the highest level job.

Kits
The idea of kits is common in all trades whereby several schedules of rates are combined into a composite schedule. Quoting one composite schedule of rates then automatically generates a series of schedules.

Latest and average costs
For materials contracts may be negotiated and purchases taken at contract rates for the life of the contract. For direct purchases the current cost will be paid. Either way the cost of stock will vary during the year and a decision has to be taken whether to charge the average cost of materials or whether to charge the latest cost (which is usually but not always higher). Generally latest costs are used because they are less complex to deal with.

Management Accounting
In general terms management accounting has a control bias. It uses similar information to financial accounting but for the purposes of budgetary planning and control, operational decisions, management information, and costing. Transactions will be analysed to enable the costs and income of the various sections of the business to be obtained for comparison. Similarly the costs of jobs, products or services need to be compared with income. The various sections of the business will need to be issued with the results of cost analyses and calculations, such as the current cost and charge rates, to enable them to function,. In addition critical success factors for the various sections need to be determined and monitored on a weekly, monthly and annual basis and used for critical decision making.

Multiple schedule of rates
It may well arise that the contractor has to agree different contracts with different customers or different areas of work for a large customer and thus has to manage several schedules of rates simultaneously.

On-costs
When calculating costs or charge rates, contractors start with the basic cost per unit and add various on-costs separately as percentages, for instance for National Insurance, administration, accommodation. In the case of charge rates a final profit percentage will be added.

Payroll costs
Payroll costs arise from the hours worked by staff and paid for. As long as non-productive hours are accounted for it should be possible to balance payroll costs closely to actual labour costs fed back to jobs and it will be important to ensure that all labour costs are accounted for as charges (preferable) or overheads. Note that the same details of hours worked are going into the payroll and the costing systems.

Profit statement
This indicates whether the business has been trading successfully or not during the time covered by the statement by comparing sales income with operating costs (receipts are ignored for this purpose.) See trading account.

Purchase orders
Purchase orders are orders placed with suppliers for goods or services. For a large organisation this is usually done through an official purchasing officer and the method of requesting the purchasing officer to place the order would be through a requisition note. It is essential to put an expenditure code and probable cost on orders to assist with their authorisation and to enable an analysis of accruals by expenditure code to be produced at period end. It will not be possible to pay the invoice without an expenditure code.

Requisition note
In a large organisation the method of purchasing goods or services may often be by placing requisitions with a purchasing officer, providing all of the details required for the purchase order.

Schedule of rates
Often known as full schedule, a schedule of rates is a list of the unit charges for carrying out an item of work in a business. It is usually made up of a combination of labour charges (from a table of labour charges by trade), material and transport charges. An example would be the labour and materials required to lay a square metre of flags or the staff time to produce a day's computer code. The charges would then be so many units of that schedule. The estimate for a complete job would be a series of work items or tasks totalled. The labour elements of work items will probably have been measured by time-and-motion study and perhaps agreed with unions. Note that there is a direct comparison with the concept of activity (job) and task (work item) in IT project management.

Standard costing
This refers to the use of schedules of rates to produce fixed estimates for jobs and feeding back the actual costs for comparison. The schedule of rates would be charged, not the actual costs.

Target hours
A combination of schedule of rates and dayworks with the staff time at schedule of rates but the materials at cost plus overheads.

Accounting Terms

Trading account
A trading account or profit/loss statement shows the gross and net profit and the outline format is: sales, less cost of sales (materials, storage, wages and salaries, stock and work-in-progress difference) to form the gross profit. From this are subtracted overheads (repairs, travel, advertising) and staffing/finance costs (cost of headquarters, services, financial charges, depreciation, administration and management) to form the net profit. Often then called the profit and loss account.

Trial balance
A statement of all debit and credit balances in the general ledger of a double entry accounting system, drawn up to test their equality, usually at period end.

Viring
The act of moving monies from one budget heading to another by agreement.

Work centre
A work centre (or depot) is the physical location of a business unit and may equate to a cost centre, just be part of it or it may contain several cost centres. A work centre will have a physical address and may be a way of allocating contracts.

12. IT TERMS

This section defines some of the almost unlimited numbers of IT terms and acronyms in use, each area having its own specialities.

IT Term	Meaning
24x7x365	24 hours a day, 7 days a week, 365 days a year
32-bit	The number of bits of information (in this case 32) dealt with by the hardware at one time
3COM	A supplier of networking equipment and associated software
3GL	Procedural computer development languages such as Cobol, Fortran, Java, C
3Ps	Progress, Problems and Plans: a good format for progress reports
486	The old standard of PC which was needed to run Windows applications efficiently, superseding the 386 microprocessor and itself replaced by the Pentium
4GL	Computer development languages such as C++ and Visual Basic designed for rapid development and which try to minimise procedural coding
7Ss	Strategy, Structure, Systems, Style, Staff, Skills, Shared values: as used in the analysis and comparison of management strategies and operational methods
Access	Microsoft's desktop database
ActiveX	A Microsoft programming language alternative to Java allowing a program to run inside a Web page
ADC	Analogue to Digital Converter: part of a sound card
ADSL	Asymmetric Digital Subscriber Line which converts a standard telephone line to carry video, CD quality sound, fast Internet access etc
AGP	Advanced Graphics Port: for fast graphics cards
AI	Artificial Intelligence: the simulation of human thoughts and reasoning, eg Expert Systems
AltaVista	An Internet search engine
AM	Amplitude Modulation whereby a transmission wave is modulated by its size (see FM)
Analogue	The wave form, as opposed to digital, method of transmitting signals over wires or by air
ANSI	The American National Standards Institute which sets IT standards
AOL	America OnLine: a large online service and Internet provider
APACS	The Association of Payments and Clearing Systems which sets bank cheque standards
APB	All Points Bulletin: a network message to all users
API	Applications Programming Interface which enables programmers to use built-in Windows functions
Applet	A small program which can be embedded within HTML to produce animation etc

IT Terms

Application	The program on a computer which carries out the functions a user requires, such as word processing or property repairs
Archiving	The saving of historical data on to a cheap but reliable medium for long term retention
ARPANet	A wide area network set up by the US Government Advanced Research Projects Agency in 1969 for defence purposes and which spawned the Internet in 1982, and was subsequently opened up to non-government and non-academic users in 1989
ASCII	American Standard Code for Information Interchange which is one of two major ways of holding characters as bits and accessible by all computers (see EBCDIC)
ASP	Proprietary Microsoft scripting technology which allows easy access to Microsoft Access databases, producing dynamic HTML pages
ASP	Application Service Provider: offers web services
Asynchronous	A process which can occur without having to synchronise with another process; generally slower than synchronous
ATM	Automatic Teller Machine: a 'hole-in-the-wall' cash machine
ATM	Asynchronous Transfer Mode which is the fast (1Gb/sec) and flexible wide area networking standard that many large installations are moving to and which can accommodate voice, data, video and image traffic
Audit trail	The ability to trace a sequence of events and the source of those events
Audit	A check on the management and effectiveness of a set of tasks
Back-up	The saving of hard disk data to external media to enable it to be kept safe in case of serious system failure
BACS	The Bankers Automated Clearing Services system which is used for instance to pay staff and invoices and by customers to pay for services; transactions are collected on day 1, processed on day 2 and made available to accounts on day 3
Bandwidth	The amount of information that can be transferred per second; for example 56Kb/s means 56 times 1024 bits per second. (about 500 characters/sec)
Bar code	A way of representing characters as easily machine-readable marks on paper
BASIC	Beginners All-purpose Symbolic Instruction Code which is a simplified form of Fortran invented in 1964 but still a powerful programming language
Batch systems	Off-line systems which usually run at night to carry out the bulk processing of data
BCS	British Computer Society which is the UK body setting standards for IT professionals
Benchmark	An attempt to model the performance of an application, software, or hardware against criteria, using the software and hardware to be employed and typical large scale data and simulated transactions
BIOS	Basic Input-Output System which is the software controlling the basic data transfer functions of a PC
Bit	A Binary Digit which is the smallest amount of data in a computer, set at 0 or 1 (off or on)
Bit-map	A pattern of bits forming an image; a simple way to hold graphics

Boot sector	An area of hard disk which holds the start-up software
Boot	To start up a computer, automatically loading in the essential basic software
Bps	Bits per second
Bridge	A way to link two Local Area Networks
Browser	Software which allows the display of web pages and enables links to other pages (which may not be in the same site); such as Netscape Navigator and Microsoft Internet Explorer
BS5750	The British standard for quality products and services (see ISO9000)
BSI	British Standards Institute which is the British equivalent of ANSII
BT	British Telecommunications, the UK's largest telecommunications, telephone and cabling company
Bubble-jet printer	Similar to an ink-jet printer
Bug	A logical error in a program
Bulletin board	All electronic notice board on a network
Bus	The hard wired communication path for data, programs and commands between major components of a computer such as processor and memory, or between computers in a local area network
Business analysis	The understanding, analysis and documentation of business processes and their shortcomings, and the identification of improvements
Business model	A representation of an organisation's structure, information stores and communication channels
Business objectives	What a business wishes to achieve
Business Process Review (BPR)	The review of existing business processes to identify shortcomings and look for more effective ways of carrying out procedures
Business processes	The activities an organisation carries out to meet its needs
Button	An iconised part of a Windows screen enabling functions to be initiated with one mouse click
Byte	Eight bits which is the computer storage required to hold one character generally
C	A high level simple but efficient language used for the production of systems software, originally on Unix but now on most platforms
C++	A popular object-oriented programming language based on C
Caching	A mechanism that supports the reading of information in bulk from a slow device to buffer RAM in order to improve performance
CAD	Computer Aided Drawing which is software to assist architects and engineers with design
CAM	Computer Aided Manufacturing which is software to drive a manufacturing process
CASE	Computer Aided Systems Engineering which is the general term given to using software in the analysis and design of systems
CBT	Computer-based training

IT Terms

CCITT	The International Telegraph and Telephone Consultative Committee which is an international standards body
CCT	Compulsory Competitive Tendering
CCTA	Central Computer and Telecommunications Agency (government sponsored)
CCTV	Closed Circuit Television which is used for security purposes
CD	Compact Disk which is used for music and from which the CD-ROM was developed
CD-R	Recordable CD or CD-ROM which can be used for music, video, archiving
CD-RW	Rewritable CD or CD-ROM which can be used for music, video, archiving but which is also re-usable
CD-ROM	Compact Disk Read-only memory disk capable of holding up to 600mb of data in digital form, including programs, data, audio, images and video
CGA	Colour Graphics Adaptor which is a card used to drive a PC monitor
CGI	Common Gateway Interface which is a script to enable access from an intranet to data in other servers and which formats that data into HTML for display
CHAPS	The Clearing House Automated Payments System enabling same-day financial transactions to take place, as opposed to the three day BACS system
Character	A single occurrence of an alphanumeric character or digit.
Check digit	An extra digit (number or character) added to the end of a reference number to enable the detection of corruption of the reference (which only assures to a percentage which depends on the methodology used)
Check-sum	A technique of attempting to ensure the validity of data on a file by summing fields numerically and checking against previously calculated sums held at the end of the file
Chip	A silicon or other wafer containing electronic circuits into which storage, logical and arithmetic functions can be built to use in computers
CHUI	Character User Interface (chewy), that is a text screen for users, as opposed to a GUI
CISC	Complex Instruction Set Computer chip which has a more complex set of instructions than RISC and which leads to smaller and usually more efficient programs
Client-server	A technique of moving some of the processing away from the mainframe, Unix box or PC fileserver on to the desktop PC which becomes the client, the server being the data end on the mainframe, Unix box or PC fileserver
CMOS RAM	An area which holds information about peripherals and is permanently powered by its own long-life battery
COBOL	Common Business Oriented Language traditionally used for 3GL commercial business programming and available on most machines
COLD	Computer Output to Laser Disk, for example for archiving
Colossus	The first computer, conceived at Bletchley Park and built by the Post Office in 1943, used for code-breaking
COM	Computer Output to Microfiche/Microfilm
Compiler	Software that accepts a programming language such as Cobol to generate machine code

CompuServe	A large Internet service provider
Computer	An electronic machine capable of reading, storing, processing and outputting data
CONFIG.SYS	A configuration file on a PC used to load device drivers on start up
Control totals	A method of automatically or manually ensuring that financial systems which communicate with each other remain in balance
Cookies	Pieces of software planted on to a user's hard disk to provide a service supplier with information about the user's actions and identity
Cost-benefit analysis	A means of structuring a decision on an investment by identifying and analysing the benefits and the costs of systems or proposals for comparison
CPA	Critical Path Analysis which is a project management technique
CPU	Central Processing Unit which is the central logic and arithmetical processing unit in a computer
CSSA	Computer Services and Software Association (government sponsored)
Cursor	A moveable pointer on a PC screen which can be used to change the current typing position through a mouse or arrow key, or trigger a function on the screen through the use of the mouse button or a keyboard key
DARPA	The Defense Advanced Research Projects Agency in the USA
DAT	Digital Audio Tape: high capacity data format often used to back up data
Data compression	A technique of increasing the amount of data which can be held in a given amount of storage
Data dictionary	Describes the data held in a database (which is essential for a distributed database) and often describes the surrounding processes
Data mart	A departmental data warehouse
Data mining	Searching through the data in a data warehouse to retrieve management information
Data Protection Act	The legislation covering access and management of personal computer data
Data warehouse	A large database into which detailed management information for the whole organisation is collected from operational databases for analysis
Data	Information held on computer files which is processed by the computer, such as name and address
Database	A collection of linked and indexed computer files, each file holding data of one type
DBMS	Database Management System (ie database software)
DDE	Dynamic Data Exchange is a method of exchanging data instantly between Windows applications running in the same session
DDL	Data Description Language: a standard for database description
Debug	The process of finding and clearing errors in computer programs
Decision table	A method of holding a set of rules and actions as a matrix
DES	Data Encryption Standard
Development	The coding and testing of computer programs
Dial-up	Connecting to a network by dialling in on a telephone line
Digital signature	An electronic way of verifying the identity of an Internet user through the use of an encrypted user identity

IT Terms

Digitiser	A device used to input drawings and maps by recording feature boundaries
DIP	Document Image Processing: the capture, storage and retrieval of written and typed documents and diagrams etc in graphical format
DLL	Dynamic Linked Library
DMA	Direct Memory Access: direct transfer of data between hard disk and RAM
DOS	The Disk Operating System for PCs, preceding Windows
Dot matrix printer	An inexpensive printer which produces its print through hammers striking pins on to typewriter ribbons
Downsizing	The migration of applications from one piece of hardware/software to another smaller set, usually driven by a need for cheaper hardware
Driver	A device (hardware and/or software) which acts as a protocol converter to link a service
DSP	Digital Signal Processor: a chip which can be used to convert text to speech
DSS	Decision Support System: a database with management information software, which combined with spreadsheets, graphics, and statistical and modelling packages provides managers with information for decision making
DTI	Department of Trade and Industry
DTP	Desk Top Publishing: packages with improved layout and graphical facilities over word-processing packages
DVD	Digital Versatile Disc: the multi-layered CD system holding 18Gb of data and able to support full-length films
EBCDIC	Extended Binary Coded Decimal Interchange Code ('epsedik'): one of two major ways of holding characters as bits (see ASCII)
e-commerce	Electronic commerce, particularly over the Internet
EDI	Electronic Data Interchange: the interchange of data electronically between suppliers, customers, banks, Inland Revenue etc, for example BACS
EDO-RAM	Extended Data Out RAM: faster than conventional RAM
EFT	Electronic Funds Transfer: the electronic movement of money between two organisations using EDI
EIDE	Extended Integrated Drive Electronics: a standard for hard disk drives allowing more than the 540mb limit of IDE
EIS	Executive Information System: software which enables managers without technical knowledge to produce summary management information, including in graphical form with the ability to drill down to lower levels of information
Electronic mail (email)	A means of communicating messages, text, graphics and files between users electronically, for example on the Internet, intranets, local area networks, wide area networks
EMU	European Monetary Unit
EN29000	The European standard for quality products and services (see ISO9000)
Encryption	A technique for preventing unauthorised access to sensitive data by encoding it, that is the data is converted so that the original characters are apparently randomly changed to others; when using encryption for networks the encryption is carried out with a freely-available public key (which cannot decrypt the message) and decrypted by the recipient using a unique private key (see RSA)

EPOS	Electronic Point of Sale: an electronic cash register making use of laser scanning of bar-coded product codes and hence names and prices, storing the data for transmission to central accounting facilities
Escrow	An arrangement whereby valuable data such as computer source code for a package is lodged with a third party in case the supplier goes out of business
Ethernet	A Local Area Networks structure based on a bus, devices being linked by coaxial cable
Excel	Microsoft's desktop spreadsheet
Excite	A web search engine
Expert system	A system which gathers together experience of a particular topic to enable decisions to be make about the likelihood of something being true based on given data; it consists of a knowledge base holding the data and an inference engine to search though the knowledge
Explorer	Web browser; also Microsoft's Windows file manager
Facilities management	The outsourcing of all operational and development functions to an outside company
FAQ	Frequently Asked Questions: software and hardware suppliers, and web sites, often make one available with answers to common questions
FAST	Federation Against Software Theft
Fat client	A client-server technique whereby most of the processing takes place on the PC or workstation
FAX	Facsimile transmission
FDDI	Fibre Distributed Data Interface: fibre optic cable network ANSII standard
Feasibility study	A cost-benefit study and analysis to determine the viability of a request or proposal
Fibre optic cable	A very fast network cable of glass fibre which transmits data through light pulses at a rate of 100 megabits or more per second
Field	A piece of data within a file in date, number, character, graphic or other format
File	A physical store of information usually on magnetic disk and which contains records
Fileserver	A powerful PC holding most of the databases for shared use over a local area network
Firewall	Hardware/software used to protect an organisation's network from unauthorised access to or from external networks including the Internet, and from viruses
Firmware	Software stored in hardware which may be replaced by a later version
Floating point	A means of holding large numbers in computers efficiently by holding the number of decimal places separately
Floppy disk	A removable PC disk usually holding up to 1.4 megabytes of data on a 3.5 inch disk and used for transferring programs and data between computers or for backups
FM	Frequency Modulation whereby a transmission wave is modulated by its frequency (see AM)
Footer	Space at the bottom of a printed page which can be used to hold standard data such as page number, date, file name, document name

IT Terms

Fortran	Formula Translation language invented in 1957, mainly used by engineers and scientists
Fourth Generation Language	See 4GL
FoxPro	A 4GL capable of generating applications which can run within Windows
FreeBSD	A free version of the Unix operating system
Freeserve	A large Internet service provider
Freeware	Free software
Frig	A scientific term dating from wartime electronics and engineering. A temporary get-around for a problem or for a special need
Front-end processor	A small computer running in front of a main processor to take some of the strain of network communications
FS-VDSL	Full Service Very high speed Digital Subscriber Line
FTP	File Transfer Protocol: a TCP/IP standard for transferring files between computers
FUD	Fear, Uncertainty, Doubt which is a phrase sometimes used to describe the state of mind generated in customers by dominant IT companies
Function keys	Keys on a keyboard which can be programmed to carry out commonly-used tasks
Functional Requirements Specification	The formal written specification of a particular set of business needs (FRS)
Gantt chart	A bar chart of activities and tasks and their dependence plotted against time and showing the staff resources required against tasks
Gateway	A piece of software which handles the interfaces between different networks
Gb	Gigabyte: a thousand million bytes (approximately)
GIF	Graphical Interchange Format which is a proprietary compression format, commonly found on the Internet, especially used for graphics (but not photographs-see JPEG)
GIS	Geographical Information Systems: often based on Ordnance Survey maps and provide data input, storage, retrieval and mapping facilities and are capable of relating data spatially to support decision-making activities; used for example for land searches and by the emergency services
GNVQ	General National Vocational Qualification: similar to NVQ but with a broader basis and including key skills (communications, application of number, information technology, working with others, problem solving, improving own learning and performance)
Google	An Internet search engine
Gopher	An older Internet utility (a 'go for')used to search the web for a particular subject
GPRS	General Packet Radio Services used to give mobile phones a permanent link to the Internet
GUI	Graphical User Interface (Gooey) such as Windows or X-Windows
Handshaking	The initial communication between devices across a network to establish contact and agree common protocols
Hard disk	A fixed (usually) disk capable of holding large volumes of data and programs

Hardware	The physical parts of computers such as the processor, printer, keyboard, mouse, monitor, disk drive, DAT drive, CD-ROM drive, ZIP drive etc
Hash total	A value calculated from a particular field in a record such as a reference number held in a totals record which enables detection of loss of, or corruption to, a field by comparison with a re-addition of the field from each record
Header	Space at the top of a printed page to hold standard data such as document name, chapter name
Hexadecimal	Numbers to base 16, two of which make up a byte
Hierarchical database	A database in which records are owned by others and which themselves own other records
HIPO	Hierarchical Input-Process-Output is a way of representing and breaking procedural or project tasks down to lower levels
Hotmail	Microsoft email
HTML	HyperText Mark-up Language used to create web pages
HTTP	HyperText Transfer Protocol which is the Internet protocol used to manage communication between browsers and web servers
Hub	A plug panel to link the physical sockets on a structured network into the local area network communications hardware
Hypertext	A text format which allows links to be made within and between documents
Icon	A pictorial representation on a Windows application representing a program or function
IEEE	The Institute of Electrical and Electronic Engineers
IIP	Investors In People which is a quality standard for managing human resources with emphasis on the training and development of employees
iMac	The stylish 1998 desktop Apple Macintosh
IMAP	Internet Message Access Protocol which is an email access protocol with features superior to POP3
Indexed sequential	A term applied to computer files which are basically files of sequential records but with one or more indexes into them
Informix	A major player in the large relational database field
Ingres	A major player in the large relational database field
Inkjet printer	The inkjet or bubble-jet printer produces its print by spraying ink on to the paper; usually in colour
Integer	A whole number
Intel	A major supplier of micro-processor chips
Interactive CD-ROM	Multi-media CD-ROM used for training through interactive questions, choices and answers
Internet	The world-wide network originally used to link university networks and fileservers and now used commercially; based on TCP/IP protocols and designed to have common access standards; used to display web pages and convey email
Intranet	The equivalent of the Internet used for communications within an organisation (such as sharing information, file transfer, electronic mail, database access)
IP address	The physical address of any piece of equipment linked to an IP network such as the Internet (see TCP/IP)

IT Terms

IPng	A new version of TCP/IP
IPX	The Novell Local Area Networking communications protocol
IS	Information Systems (which includes IT systems)
ISA	Industry Standard Architecture: an older standard for PC expansion cards (see PCI)
ISDN	Integrated Services Digital Network which is a fast dial-up telephone network link offered by BT and others and available internationally for voice, text and graphics; suitable for short or emergency periods for long distance links; ISDN2 is the small user version with a speed up to 128k
ISO	The International Standards Organisation
ISO9000	The international standard for quality products and services (see BS5750)
ISP	Internet Service Provider, that is a company which provides access to the Internet
IT	Information Technology
ITU-T	International Telecommunications Union-Telecommunications: sets modem standards for telecommunications
JANET	The Joint Academic Network used by UK universities and research institutions
Java applet	See Applet
Java	An object-oriented programming language proprietary to Sun similar to C++, easy to learn but less efficient than C or C++; used for writing free-standing applications, mini-programs within web pages (applets), server-side generation of HTML and running on most platforms including Windows NT, Mac, Unix, Linux and proprietary
JavaScript	A simplified form of Java but still a fairly full-featured programming language used for special effects in web pages
JAZ drive	A compact portable removable disk capable of holding 1 to 2 Gb of data
JCL	Job Control Language which is a general term for a language used by operating systems to control programs and operations
JIT	Just-In-Time which is the scheduling of a product or service to arrive just in time for operational use, such as materials or training
JPEG	Joint Photographic Experts Group which is a compressed graphics file format designed for complex colour images such as photographs
JScript	The Microsoft proprietary version of JavaScript
Kb	Kilobytes which are approximately a thousand bytes (actually 1024)
Key escrow	An arrangement whereby a trusted third party holds the encryption key to sensitive data so that it could be accessed by another body in an emergency
Keyboard	Keys similar to a typewriter's for the input of characters
LAN	Local Area Network connecting a group of PCs to allow sharing of programs, data and peripherals, usually within the same building with the data held on a central fileserver, enabling data to be centrally archived, providing email, and centralised software and security level management
Laptop	A compact, portable PC
Laser printer	A printer which uses a laser beam to produce high-resolution printed output
LCD projector	A transparent Liquid Crystal Diode screen which can be linked to a PC for projecting presentations

LED	Light Emitting Diode
Light pen	An electronic pen which is able to read bar-codes
Linux	A freely-available Unix-like operating system, which is modular, reliable and easy to use, often used for fileservers
Lotus Notes	A versatile database and data sharing package
LS120	An alternative to a floppy drive with a capacity of 120mb; can read a floppy
Lycos	An Internet search engine
Mac OS	The 1984 Apple Macintosh operating system famous for its easy-to-use graphical user interface and which inspired Windows
Mac OS X	The new 2001 Apple Macintosh operating system based on a Unix variant and incorporating advanced DVD features
Machine code	The code that computer hardware understands in order to execute an application
Macro	A short sequence of computer instructions eg to enable toolbar buttons, menus and keys to carry out operations through a single user action; many are supplied with Windows software but macros can usually also be generated by recording user actions
Mailbox	An electronic postbox containing incoming mail messages
Mb	Megabyte which is a million bytes (approximately)
MCI	Media Control Interface: eg for CD music, audio, MIDI
Memory	The rapid access storage in a computer used to hold programs and data for fast access
Meta data	Data describing the attributes of data in a database such as structure, contents, status, source, how it has been transformed
Mflops	Millions of floating point operations per second
MICR	Magnetic Ink Character Recognition, as used on the bottom of cheques
Microfiche	The recording of computer output (usually print) on film cards in a very compressed format enabling many pages per card (such as 270 A4 pages), used for archiving, searching and viewing
Microfilm	The recording of printed data on 35mm film in a compressed format for archiving, searching and viewing
Microprocessor	The computer chip in a PC which carries out the logical and arithmetic processes of a program
Microsoft Office	The Microsoft integrated office suite for the PC which may include Word, Excel, Access, PowerPoint, Schedule+, Publisher, FrontPage, Small Business Tools
Microsoft	A leading supplier of PC software including Windows, Microsoft Office, Explorer, Project
Middleware	Software which is used to link clients to servers.
MIDI	Musical Instrument Digital Interface which is a standard for controlling sound cards and electronic musical instruments
Millennium bug	Potential faults in programs due to storing or handling dates without the century
Mips	Millions of instructions per second

IT Terms

MIS	Management Information System: management reporting software which enables data to be extracted from databases and stores, and managers' reports to be produced (see DSS)
MMX	Multimedia version of the Pentium chip
Modem	Modulator/Demodulator which is hardware (such as a card) that lets the PC communicate with other computers over a phone line by converting digital signals into analogue
Module	A program procedure which performs one or more discreet functions
Monitor	The visual display unit or screen which is connected to a computer to display its contents
Mouse	A way of controlling the cursor on a PC screen, as an alternative to keys
MP3	Sound compression format, now a standard on the Internet for downloading music; part of MPEG
MPEG	Motion Picture Experts Group which is a compressed format of graphics files for use in moving pictures, video, cable, Internet
MPEG-4	Movie quality digital standard
MPP	Massively Parallel Processing which is a computer architecture which uses large arrays of CPUs that carry out processing in a parallel manner
MS-DOS	Microsoft Disk Operating System, now superseded by Windows
MTBF	Mean Time Before Failure (of hardware)
Multimedia	Computer processing of text, graphical, audio and video data
Multiplexor	A device allowing several signals to use the same line
Multiprogramming	An older term for multitasking
Multitasking	The ability of a computer to carry out more than one task simultaneously
Multithreading	The ability of a computer to process tasks apparently simultaneously by dealing with each task as a separate thread and allowing one task to overtake another if necessary
NC	Network Computer which is a cheaper computer than a PC, lacking extensive local storage and particularly suited to networks
NCC	National Computing Centre in Manchester, a centre of expertise
Netscape Navigator	A web browser
Network database	A database which is similar to a hierarchical one but with extra links between appropriate records to create quick ways of navigating across the database
Network	The connection of computer systems by communications channels and software
Newsgroup	Areas of the Internet organised by discussion group
Node	A device on a network or more often a routing centre on a network
NOS	Network Operating System such as Windows NT, Novell Netware, Macintosh OS, Unix, Linux
Novell Netware	Common local area network software in use
NT	See Windows NT

NVQ	National Vocational Qualification: UK national standards based on those developed by industry and commerce for various subjects such as IT and management, and for which the Training and Enterprise Council (TEC) is responsible; they are designed to provide qualifications for particular jobs or professions; the five levels are: 1-foundation, 2-good GCSEs, 3-'A' Levels, 4-degree, 5-post graduate; also see GNVQ
OAS	Office Automation Systems such as word processing, electronic mail, diaries
OCR	Optical Character Recognition which is machine reading of text from paper documents by optical and electronic scanning followed by software interpretation of the characters
OCR-B	The European standard for OCR which includes lower case and special symbols
ODBC	Open Database Connectivity: a standard programming interface that enables applications to access structured database management systems that use standard SQL
Office	See Microsoft Office
OLAP	On-Line Analytical Processing which is on-line data warehouse analysis
OLE	Object Linking and Embedding which is a method of opening one Windows application while in another
OMR	Optical Mark Recognition: the optical reading of printed marks for machine control purposes
OOP	Object-Oriented Programming which is high-level programming whereby objects have defined characteristics which can be inherited by other objects created from them and on which operations may be performed
Open source	Some applications come with the source code with freedom to amend it
Open Systems	The IT strategy which promotes the idea of a freedom to choose between suppliers for all elements of producing, purchasing, implementing and running computer applications
Operating system	Software which allows operators, computer programs and computer hardware to communicate with each other
Oracle	A major player in the large relational database field
OSI	Open Systems Interconnection: the seven layer standard for communication between systems: Application, Presentation, Session, Transport, Network, Datalink, Physical, eg TCP/IP
PABX	Private Automatic Branch Exchange: private automatic telephone exchange
Packet	In information transfer on networks data is often broken into entities called packets, each with its destination and source addresses; users pay for packets rather than line time
PAF	The Post Office Address File containing all postal delivery addresses for the whole of the UK and from which the postcode can be extracted or the address generated from the postcode and house number
Parallel running	The technique of running a new computer application using the same data as the old one and reconciling the results
Parity bit	A bit added to characters used to detect data transfer or transmission errors
Patch	A temporary amendment to software to fix a fault, to get around a fault or to produce a special version of the software

IT Terms

PC	Personal Computer which is a small desktop computer consisting of processor, monitor, disk drives, keyboard, mouse etc
PCI	Peripheral Component Interconnect: deals with PC graphics faster than ISA
PDF	Portable Document File: a standard for documents in book format
PDW	Project Definition Workshop which is a meeting used to formally initiate a project, to define the objectives of the project and to gain commitment
Pentium	Intel copyright name for the generation of micro processor after a 486; other suppliers refer to their equivalents as 586s
Performance indicators	Ways to set and measure the delivery of a service or competency
Perl	A scripting language
Pert	A powerful yet easy-to-learn programming language often used for servers and the production of web pages
PERT	Programme Evaluation and Review Technique which is a project network analysis methodology which can be used to find the critical path of a project
PGP	Pretty Good Privacy which is a free implementation of public key encryption whereby information is encoded with a publicly-available encryption key which can then be decoded only with a private key; in PGP only the key is asymmetrically encoded, the data being symmetrically encoded for simplicity (see RSA)
Pilot runs	A technique of minimising the risks of a new computer application by running it initially for just a part of the business
PIN	Personal Identification Number which is a number allocated to a person enabling them to authorise transactions such as those used in cash machines and mobile phones
Pixel	Picture element: the dots on monitors etc which make up the image
PnP	Plug and Play: modern PCs have a BIOS able to recognise hardware added
Polling	In networking, the act of checking each communications line in sequence to see if a message is waiting to come in from a terminal
POP	Post Office Protocol as used for web-based emailing
POP3	Post Office Protocol 3 as used for non-web based emailing and hence allowing off-line working and outgoing message queuing
Port	A physical socket or other connector on a computer (with its attendant firmware) allowing it to link to external devices and networks
Post-implementation review	The formal review of a project some months after its implementation to measure its success against the objectives set and to give feedback on successes and failures
PowerPoint	Microsoft's presentation graphics package
Presentation graphics	Software to enable the production of business presentations (an improvement on overhead slides)
PRINCE	Project In Controlled Environment which is a methodology for information systems project management, especially used by government agencies

Private key	The private key in encryption is the key consisting of the two prime numbers (whose product forms the public key) and which is used by an individual to decrypt data which has been encoded by using a public key specific to that person; or the private key can be used to send and prove a digital signature visible to all via the public key (see PGP also)
Program	A series of instructions in a computer used to carry out operations
Project management	The planning, monitoring, controlling and reporting on the activities and tasks necessary to carry out a project
Project Manager	For a larger project a full time post involved in planning, controlling and reporting on activities and tasks in a project, reporting to the Project Sponsor
Project plan	The activities and tasks necessary to implement a system and the relationships between them, tasks having estimates of size and the resources to carry them out
Project Review Board	A small group of expertise used by the Project Sponsor to review the progress of a project against the plan and to provide advice
Project Sponsor	The owner of a project with overall responsibility for its success
Protocol	An agreed set of rules, for example for network communications
Prototyping	The development of an application using a 4GL in close liaison with the user to ensure continuous agreement on the evolution of the product
PSS	Packet Switching System which is BT's long-distance networking system
PSTN	Public Switched Telephone Network
PSU	Power Supply Unit
Public key	Public key encryption is where information is encoded with a public key which is specific to the person being sent the message and which is freely available but which can only be decrypted with the private key held by that person; or it can be used to read a digital signature encrypted by an individual's private key; it consists of the product of the two large prime numbers which themselves form the private key (see PGP also)
Quality Assurance	QA is an activity carried out by a supplier to independently assure the quality of a product
Qwerty	The name given to the standard layout of english language keyboards
RAM	Random Access Memory on PCs used to hold currently active applications and data
RDBMS	Relational Database Management System: a flexible database format consisting of tables of data whose items can be related and indexed through keys; different views of the same data can be presented to different users according to their needs; the standard for Unix systems of large size and PC fileservers, and replacing hierarchical and networked databases
RDF	Resource Description Framework as used to define Internet data
Record	A collection of fields holding one type of data
Relational database	See RDBMS
RISC	Reduced Instruction Set Computer chip which is cheaper than CISC with a simplified set of instructions but may be less efficient
Risk management	The identification and management of the risks associated with a project
ROM	Non-volatile Read Only Memory on PCs used to hold system programs

IT Terms

Router	Intelligent software and hardware which links networks and which despatches messages over the best route currently available and blocks unnecessary messages
RS232	An ANSII standard for serial interfaces
RSA	A cipher methodology consisting of asymmetrical keys invented in the USA by Rivest, Shamir and Adleman which removed the need to pass a key with an encrypted message; originally invented in the UK but not exploited (see public and private keys and PGP)
Scanner	A combination of hardware and software which can read text or graphics from paper into a computer
Scoping	The process of assessing the impact of a proposal, including its limits, the costs, resources, timescales, risks
Script	Short programs used to test the performance of a system against expected results, or to carry out standard operations
SCSI	Small Computer System Interface (skuzzy) which is a fast, standard, general-purpose asynchronous serial port for hard drives, tape, DAT, CD-ROM, ZIP drive; it can daisy-chain peripherals
SCSI-2	Synchronous data transfer, faster than SCSI
SD-RAM	Synchronous Dynamic RAM: faster than EDO-RAM
Search engine	Software that searches Internet web sites for given keywords
Server	A general term used for software/hardware which provides a particular service; for example a fileserver is a powerful PC dedicated to holding data on a local area network or on the Internet; an email server is software managing the email database
SIMM	Single Inline Memory Module: a standard type of circuit board containing RAM memory chips.
SLA	Service Level Agreement for services between a customer and an internal or external supplier
Smart card	A credit card sized card containing a chip with data, and confidential and secret sections
SMART	Specific, Measurable, Achievable, Results-oriented, Time-limited: as applied to the production of decision criteria or the benefits of proposals
Smartsuite	The Lotus integrated suite of PC software which may include WordPro, Lotus 123, Approach, Freelance Graphics and Organiser
SMOG	Simplified Measure of Gobbledegook: a measure of the simplicity of prose
Software	The computer programs which drive a computer
Source language	The language (usually English-like) in which a program is written
Spam	Unsolicited emails produced in large volume
Spooling	The process of producing print images on disk or tape for later printing
Spreadsheet	An electronic version of an accountant's spreadsheet with automatic totalling, formulae etc
SQL	Structured Query Language: a standard for communicating with relational databases in an English-like way
SSADM	Structured Systems Analysis and Design Methodology which was developed by a government agency and which is obligatory in government contracts
STP	Shielded Twisted Pair

Structured cabling	The installation of communication cabling points around offices which allows flexible positioning and movement of PCs, printers and phones (see UTP5) Structured Programming using standard control structures such as 'do sequence of programming operations', 'if-then-else', 'while loop', decision tables
SVGA	Super VGA which is a screen resolution giving better screen definition than VGA
SWIFT	Society of World-wide International Financial Telecommunications
Switch	Allows a PC to have a faster link to a fileserver where the local area network traffic is heavy, for example for GIS
SWOT	Strengths, Weaknesses, Opportunities and Threats: as used in the analysis of personal attributes or organisation goals
Sybase	A major player in the large relational database field
Synchronous	A process that has to wait for another process to complete before it can be carried out: generally faster than asynchronous
System Specification	The detailed specification of a computer system to meet the business needs of a user, derived from the functional requirements specification
System X	BT's digital telephone exchange system now standard throughout the UK
System	A collection of programs carrying out related functions
Systems analysis	The analysis of requirements to convert a business need into a computer system
Systems engineering	The investigation, computer modelling and redevelopment of complex systems
Systems software	All software other than the application software; used to carry out standard functions
Systems trials	The testing of computer programs when linked together to ensure that the system meets the agreed specification
Table	A representation of data in a relational database whereby the data is arranged as rows and columns; a row is equivalent to a record and a column to a field
Talk21	BT domestic free email
TCP/IP	Transport Control Protocol/Internet Protocol which is the communications protocol commonly used with Unix and used on the Internet
Teleworking	Using a computer remotely from the office, such as from home, to carry out one's job
TelNet	A protocol for computers to communicate with each other
Terminal	A simple form of workstation which does not have the capability of a PC
Thermal printer	An older form of printer using heat to produce characters on special paper
Thin client	A client-server technique whereby most of the processing takes place at the server, for example in an Network Computer
TickIT	The quality standard for software within the framework of ISO9000
Token Ring	A local area network structure in which tokens are passed to transfer data
Toolbar	A collection of iconised buttons in Windows enabling actions to be carried out with one key-press as an alternative to using the menus
TP	TeleProcessing: the generic term for mainframe on-line systems
TQM	Total Quality Management: a USA term for overall quality management
Trackball	An attachment to a laptop PC which acts similarly to a mouse

IT Terms

TTY	Teletype which is an old way of driving printers (they were originally modified typewriters)
Unix	An operating system and related hardware first produced by AT&T in 1970 and widely used by academics, which has become an open standard produced by most suppliers and which is considered to be a stable platform
UOM	Unit of Measure, for example square metres
UPS	Uninteruptable Power Supply
URL	Uniform Resource Locator which is the address of a web site consisting of the protocol (eg http://), host (eg www.bbc.co.uk) and file path (eg /radio4)
USB	Universal Serial Bus: an alternative to parallel and serial ports allowing up to 127 peripherals to be connected
User acceptance trials	Following systems trials and quality assurance trials, the supplier of a new system will hand the system over for the users to ensure that it meets the agreed specification before going live
User Group	An organisation of users of a particular product who share experiences, lobby for improvements and fund enhancements
User guide	A detailed manual on how to use an IT application or piece of hardware
UTP5	Unshielded Twisted Pair level 5: a structured cabling standard
V90	The ITU-T standard for 56k modems
VAR	Value-Added Reseller which is any organisation adding value to a product or service and then re-selling it
VBA	Visual Basic for Applications
VBS	Visual Basic Script
VDU	Visual Display Unit: see monitor
VGA	Video Graphics Array which is a standard for screen definition (see SVGA)
Video conferencing	Linking groups of people in remote offices with vision, sound, whiteboard and file transfer facilities on networked workstations
Virus	An unwanted piece of program code which copies itself and may cause loss of data or facilities
Visual Basic	A Windows 4GL used to produce PC applications or front-end existing mainframe and Unix applications and thus convert them to Windows-like systems
Voicemail	A facility provided by electronic telephone exchanges to record messages from callers, similar to an answering machine
VRAM	Video RAM: fast RAM with separate input and output buses
W3C	World Wide Web Committee which is the Internet standards organisation
Walkthrough	Using a small working group to check out a user requirement or system defined on paper to try to ensure its viability before further commitment by going through its workings
WAN	Wide Area Network which is the linking of local area networks in remote sites by means a fast network, often on leased lines or fibre optic cables
WAP	Wireless Application Protocol which is a version of XML used for video conferencing, and to allow access to the Internet from mobile phones to view stripped-down web pages and email

Web	The Internet was extended to graphical web pages in 1989 through the designs of Tim Berners-Lee
Web page	Pages of information structured in HTML which is accessible by a browser
Web site	A fileserver running HTTP programs enabling web pages to be accessed
Webcam	A web camera giving continual web pictures from a site
Windows 2000	The millennium release of Windows
Windows 95	A release of Windows desktop software which allows multi-tasking
Windows 98	The 1998 release of desktop Windows, aligned to Internet working
Windows NT	Windows New Technology, which is a version of the Windows operating system used across networks and competes with Unix; more secure and stable than other versions; consists of NT Workstation and NT Server
Windows	The graphical operating system which allows easier use of DOS-type functions
WinZip	Windows version of the PC file compression tool used to save space
Word processor	An electronic 'typewriter' which saves the words entered on to disk to enable subsequent amendment and reprinting
Word	Microsoft's word processor
Work agreement	A formal agreement between two parties within an organisation to carry out given tasks at a particular cost and timescale
Workstation	A PC or other device which gives access to a computer
World Wide Web (WWW)	The Web is a network of linked file servers setting a standard for interactive graphical displays on the Internet, and providing a series of multi-media documents containing links to other sources of information
Worm	A type of virus
WORM	Write Once Read Many – a storage device such as a recordable CD-ROM used for archiving for example
WP	Word Processing
WYSIWYG	What You See Is What You Get (wizziwig): what you type is the way it comes out on the screen or printer (in theory)
X/OPEN	A group setting standards for operating systems
X25	A CCITT standard for packet switched networks
X400	A CCITT standard which is widely used for electronic mail and other office automation
XHTML	Combined XML and HTML
XML	eXtensible Mark-up Language: potential multimedia successor to HTML which is more adaptable and enables data to be structured according to its type rather than solely how it should be displayed with HTML; used for video recording on hard disk and emerging as the e-commerce standard
X-WINDOWS	The open version of Windows, often used on Unix
Y2K	The year 2000 and issues related to it. See Millennium bug.
Yahoo	A web index site and search engine in which web pages are vetted and added manually
ZIP drive	A compact form of portable fixed disk holding 100 Mb or 250 Mb
ZIP	A PC file compression tool used to save space

13. BIBLIOGRAPHY

The author acknowledges his indebtedness to the following publications which were consulted for reference:

- Essential Manager's Manual, R Heller & T Hindle, Dorling Kindersley, 1998
- Information Systems in Practice, B McNurlin & R Sprague, Prentice-Hall, 1989
- ISO9000 for Small Businesses, R Tricker, Butterworth Heinemann, 1997
- Management, R. Bennett, M & E Handbooks, 1994
- Managing Computer Projects, S Price, J Wiley, 1986
- Managing Difficult People, K Mannering, How To Books, 2000
- Mastering Systems Analysis and Design, M Hughes, Macmillan, 2000
- NVQ Management Standards, Edexcel, 1999
- Practical Open Systems, I Hugo, Blackwell, 1991
- Project Management, D Lock, Gower, 1996
- Starting Your Own Business, Consumers Association, 1999
- Systems Analysis, J Bingham & G Davies, Macmillan, 1994
- Teach Yourself Intranets, N Vandome, Teach Yourself Books, 1999
- The Business Plan Workbook, C Barron, D Barron & R Brown, Kogan Page, 1998
- The Data Protection Act 1998, The Data Protection Commissioner
- The Good Manager's Guide, T Boutall, MCI, 1997
- The Manager's Book of Checklists, D Rowntree, F.T. Management, 1996
- The Manager's Handbook, A Young, Sphere, 1987
- The Office Safety Handbook, R Saunders, Pitman, 1995

The following web sites were also consulted:

British Computer Society	**http://www.bcs.org.uk**
Data Protection	**http://www.dataprotection.gov.uk**
Economics & Business Education Association	**http://www.bized.ac.uk**
Edexcel	**http://www.edexcel.org.uk**
National Computing Centre	**http://www.ncc.co.uk**
National Health Service	**http://www.imc.exec.nhs.uk**
Web standards	**http://www.w3.org**

INDEX

Symbols

24x7x365 202
32-bit 202
3COM 202
3GL 202
3Ps 202
4GL 202
7Ss 202

A

Access 202
Access level control security 93
Access to source code security 94
Accountancy codes 197
Accounting period 197
ACCOUNTing TERMS 197
Accruals 197
ActiveX 202
Activity/task monitor 61
Actual costs 197
ADC 202
Administration areas 179
ADMINISTRATION, FINANCE AND PROPERTY 179
Administration Procedures 179
ADSL 202
Advertising for staff 161
Agenda format 31
AGP 202
AI 202
AltaVista 202
AM 202
Analogue 202
ANSI 202
AOL 202
APACS 202
APB 202
API 202
Applet 202
Application 203
Application requirements 81, 117
Application software 121
Appraisal of Managers 158
Appraisal outline 154
Appraising staff 170
Appraising yourself 170
Archiving 203
ARPANet 203
ASCII 203
ASP 203
Assertiveness 173
Asynchronous 203
ATM 203
Audit 203
Audit trail 203
Audit trails 94

B

Back-up 203
Backup and recovery 122
BACS 203
Bad news communication 24
Balance sheet 197
Bandwidth 203
Bar code 203
Bar code standards 105
BASIC 203
Batch systems 203
BCS 203
Behaving commercially 157
Benchmark 203
Benchmark evaluation plan 128
BIOS 203
Bit 203
Bit-map 203
Boot 204
Boot sector 204
Bps 204
Bridge 204
Browser 204
BS5750 204
BSI 204
BT 204
Bubble-jet printer 204
Budget cuts 184
Budget heading 197
Budget Management 184
Budget monitoring 185
Budget preparation 184
Budgets 197
Bug 204
Building Alteration Costs 190
Building estimates/contracts 190
Building finance 189
Building labour 190
Building materials 191
Building planning 190
Bulletin board 204
Bus 204
Business Aims and Objectives 6
BUSINESS ANALYSIS 71
Business Analysis 71
Business analysis 204
Business controls 184
Business failure causes 7
Business model 204
Business objectives 204
Business plan 9
BUSINESS PLANNING 6
Business Planning 7
Business planning 159
Business Process Review 204
Business process review 72
Business processes 204
Business requirements 74, 80
Business review 8
Business start-up 176
Business structure identification 73

INDEX

Button 204
Byte 204

C

C 204
C++ 204
Caching 204
CAD 204
Call log contents 113
CAM 204
CASE 204
Cash flow statement 198
CBT 204
CCITT 205
CCT 205
CCTA 205
CCTV 205
CD 205
CD-R 205
CD-ROM 205
CD-RW 205
Centralisation advantages 18
CGA 205
CGI 205
Change approval 64
Change control security 90
Change management 47
Change planning 46
Change summary report 65
CHAPS 205
Character 205
Check digit 205
Check-sum 205
Chip 205
CISC 205
Client-server 205
Client-server advantages 88
Client-server disadvantages 88
Client-Server Issues 88
CMOS RAM 205
COBOL 205
Coding Standards 109
COLD 205
Colossus 205
COM 205
Commitments 198
Communicating with Customers 23
Company details 131
Competence scales 156
Competences
  general   155
  specific   155
Compiler 205
Complaining customers 23
Complaints analysis 44
CompuServe 206
Computer 206
CONFIG.SYS 206
Contra accounts 198
Contract contents 136

Contract guarantees 132
Contract references 131
Contracting 136
Contracts previously won 132
Control totals 198, 206
Cookies 206
Cost centre 198
Cost plus 198
Cost-benefit Analysis 76
Cost-benefit analysis 206
Costing system 198
Costs and charges 198
Costs appraisal 74
CPA 206
CPU 206
Criminal offences 97
CSSA 206
Current system appraisal 73
Curriculum Vitae 165
Cursor 206
Customer Care 21
Customer care benefits 21
CUSTOMER COMMUNICATION 21
Customer relationships 22
Customer service attitude 21
Customisation and maintenance 122

D

DARPA 206
DAT 206
Data 206
Data compression 206
Data dictionary 206
Data mart 206
Data mining 206
Data Protection Act 95, 206
Data Protection practicalities 97
Data Protection principles 95
Data retention and recovery 91
Data safeguarding 92
Data security and administration ... 119
Data warehouse 206
Database 206
Database data design 102
Database Design 102
Database proposals 121
Database standard files 102
Date standards 104
Dayworks 199
DBMS 206
DDE 206
DDL 206
Debug 206
Decentralisation advantages 18
Decentralisation of Services 18
Decision making skills 139
Decision table 206
Delegation of work 145
Departmental strategic activities 12
DES 206

Developing yourself	171
Development	206
Dial-up	206
Difficult staff	146
Digital signature	206
Digitiser	207
DIP	207
Disciplinary penalties	150
Disciplinary procedures	150
Dismissal	151
DLL	207
DMA	207
Document design	29
Documentation house style	27
Documentation update security	91
DOS	207
Dot matrix printer	207
Double entry accounting	199
Downsizing	207
Driver	207
DSP	207
DSS	207
DTI	207
DTP	207
DVD	207

E

e-commerce	207
EBCDIC	207
EDI	207
EDO-RAM	207
Effective organisations	10
EFT	207
EIDE	207
EIS	207
Electronic mail (email)	207
Email skills	25
Employees Health & Safety role	183
Empowering staff	145
EMU	207
EN29000	207
Encryption	207
EPOS	208
Escrow	208
Estimating Costs	83
Estimating Development Time	99
Ethernet	208
Excel	208
Excite	208
Expert system	208
Explorer	208

F

Facilities management	208
Factoring	199
FAQ	208
FAST	208
Fat client	208
FAX	208
FDDI	208
Feasibility report	78
Feasibility Study	78
Feasibility study	208
Feedback handling	141
Fibre optic cable	208
Field	208
File	208
File controls security	93
Fileserver	208
Financial Accounting	199
Financial Control Requirements	106
Financial controls	106
Financial information	132
Firewall	208
Firmware	208
Floating point	208
Floppy disk	208
FM	208
Footer	208
Fortran	209
Fourth Generation Language	209
FoxPro	209
FreeBSD	209
Freeserve	209
Freeware	209
Frig	209
Front-end processor	209
FS-VDSL	209
FTP	209
FUD	209
Function attendance	177
Function keys	209
Functional Requirements Specification	80, 209
Functional Requirements Specification appendices	81
Functions identification	73

G

Gantt chart	209
Gantt chart example	60
Gateway	209
Gb	209
General risks	53
Getting to know people	177
GIF	209
GIS	209
Giving orders	157
GNVQ	209
Good politics	140
Google	209
Gopher	209
GPRS	209
Grievance, Disciplinary and Dismissal	150
Grievances	150
GUI	209
Guidelines for written communications	27

INDEX

H

Handbook	35
HANDBOOK INTRODUCTION	5
Handshaking	209
Hard disk	209
Hardware	210
Hardware proposals	120
Hardware requirements	86
Hash total	210
Header	210
Health & Safety organisation	182
Health & Safety Regulations	182
Help Desk	44
Help Desk organisation	44
Help facilities	104
Hexadecimal	210
Hierarchical database	210
Hierarchical plan example	49
Hierarchical project plan	49
High achievement attainment	172
HIPO	210
Hotmail	210
HTML	210
HTML basics	37
HTML colours	38
HTTP	210
Hub	210
Hypertext	210

I

Icon	210
IEEE	210
IIP	210
iMac	210
Image management	173
IMAP	210
Implementation plan	111
Implementation Planning	110
Implementation proposals	124
Indexed sequential	210
Inefficiency management	146
Informix	210
Ingres	210
Inkjet printer	210
Intangible benefits	77
Integer	210
Intel	210
Interactive CD-ROM	210
Internal Trading Units	199
Internet	210
Internet pages	36
Interview kit	167
Interview management	168
Interview preparation	162, 166
Interview questions preparation	166
Interview questions to ask	167
Interviewing	163
Intranet	210
Intranet pages	37
Invoice payment	185
IP address	210
IPng	211
IPX	211
IS	211
ISA	211
ISDN	211
ISO	211
ISO9000	211
ISO9000 advantages	15
ISO9000 disadvantages	16
ISO9000 elements	15
ISO9000 implementation	16
ISP	211
IT	211
IT TERMS	202
ITU-T	211

J

JANET	211
Java	211
Java applet	211
JavaScript	211
JAZ drive	211
JCL	211
JIT	211
Job application completion	165
Job application rejection	169
Job application/interview tips	168
Job description formulation	160
Job description outline	161
Job follow-up call	164
Job hunting	164
Job offer	169
Job Seeking	164
Job seeking preparation	164
JPEG	211
JScript	211

K

Kb	211
Keeping ahead of competitors	11
Key escrow	211
Keyboard	211
Kits	199

L

LAN	211
Laptop	211
Laser printer	211
Latest and average costs	199
LCD projector	211
Leadership actions	144
Leadership attitude	143
LED	212
Liability insurances	132
Light pen	212

Linux 212
Listening skills 23
Lotus Notes 212
LS120 212
Lycos 212

M

Mac OS 212
Mac OS X 212
Machine code 212
Macro 212
Mailbox 212
Maintenance and Support Provision 113
Management Accounting 199
Management Functions 137
Management functions 137
Management methods 137
Management planning activities 138
Managers Competences 157
Managers competences 157
Managers Health & Safety role 183
Managing a quality service 158
Managing Activities 192
Managing change 10
Managing Energy 195
Managing Information 195
Managing Meetings 30
Managing People 194
Managing Presentations 32
Managing Projects 196
Managing projects 14
Managing Quality 196
Managing Resources 193
Managing resources 158
Managing self 158
Managing staff 158
Managing the customer relationship 13
Managing the IT organisation 13
Managing Yourself 170
Marketing methods 34
Marketing outline 34
Marketing Products and Services 34
Mb 212
MCI 212
Meetings communications 31
Meetings organisation 30
Memorandum and letter production 28
Memory 212
Menus/commands standards 104
Meta data 212
Mflops 212
MICR 212
Microfiche 212
Microfilm 212
Microprocessor 212
Microsoft 212
Microsoft Office 212
Middleware 212
MIDI 212
Milestones progress report 65

Millennium bug 212
Minutes production 31
mips 212
MIS 213
MMX 213
Modem 213
Module 213
Monitor 213
Monthly tasks for staff 43
Motivation of staff 144
Mouse 213
MP3 213
MPEG 213
MPEG-4 213
MPP 213
MS-DOS 213
MTBF 213
Multimedia 213
Multiple schedule of rates 200
Multiplexor 213
Multiprogramming 213
Multitasking 213
Multithreading 213

N

NATIONAL MANAGEMENT STANDARDS 192
NC 213
NCC 213
Negotiating skills 24
Netscape Navigator 213
Network 213
Network costs 84
Network database 213
Network proposals 120
New employee induction 180
Newsgroup 213
Newsletter 35
Node 213
NOS 213
Novell Netware 213
NT 213
NVQ 214

O

OAS 214
Objectives of an IT organisation 6
OCR 214
OCR-B 214
ODBC 214
Office 214
Office risk assessment 182
OLAP 214
OLE 214
OMR 214
On-costs 200
On-line Guidelines 103
OOP 214
Open hardware 87

Open software	87
Open source	214
Open Systems	214
Open systems areas	87
Open systems compliance	118
Open Systems Standards	87
Operating system	214
Operational areas	138
Operational release security	91
Operations estimates	84
Oracle	214
Organisation strategic activities	11
Organising projects	138
OSI	214
Outsourcing advantages	19
Outsourcing of Services	19
Outsourcing risks	19

P

PABX	214
Package acceptance criteria	128
Package Benchmarking	128
Package benchmarking	124
Package costs	125
Package documentation	121
Package Evaluation	126
Package evaluation security	91
Package installation	123
Package licensing	123
Package management reports	118
Package match scores	127
Package Proposals	120
Package Requirements	117
Package Risk Management	129
Package risks	129
Package security	122
Package selection criteria	126
Package sizing data	119
Package summary proposals	120
Package supplier viability	124
Package support	122
Package training	123
Package user base questionnaire	127
Package weightings	127
PACKAGES, TENDERS AND CONTRACTS	117
Packet	214
PAF	214
Page header standards	105
Paper files	96
Parallel running	214
Parity bit	214
Patch	214
Payroll costs	200
PC	215
PCI	215
PDF	215
PDW	215
Pentium	215
Performance Indicators	41
Performance indicators	215
Performance indicators for applications staff	42
Performance indicators for operational services	41
Performance management	146
Perl	215
Person specification	161
Persuasion skills	24
PERT	215
Pert	215
PGP	215
Pilot runs	215
PIN	215
Pixel	215
PnP	215
Politics in Management	140
Politics to be avoided	140
Polling	215
POP	215
POP3	215
Port	215
Post-implementation Review	68
Post-implementation review	215
Post-implementation review report	68
Post-implementation review terms of reference	68
Post-interview processes	163
PowerPoint	215
Presentation graphics	215
Presentation management	33
Presentation preparation	32
PRINCE	215
Printed output controls	93
Printed Output Standards	105
Private key	216
Process specification format	107
Process Specifications	107
Process specifications strategy	107
Processing personal data	95
Processing sensitive data	96
Product and Service Provision	17
Products and services to offer	17
Professional Activities	13
Profit statement	200
Program	216
Program development security	94
Progress reports	181
Project activities/tasks	60
Project approval dates	63
Project budget monitor	67
Project Budget Monitoring	67
Project cost areas	76
Project Definition Workshop agenda	56
Project Definition Workshop aims	55
Project Definition Workshop ground rules	57
Project Definition Workshop introduction	57
Project Definition Workshop preparation	56
Project file	52
Project identification	63
Project Initiation	55
Project Management	60
Project management	216
Project management elements	48
Project Management Roles	58

Project Management Summary 48
Project management tips 60
Project Manager 216
Project Manager role 58
Project managers 63
Project plan 216
Project plan activities 51
Project plan attributes 50
Project plan bad news 62
Project plan example 50
Project plan progress report contents 61
Project Planning 50
Project Planning and Management 45
Project profit monitor 69
Project resource analysis 69
Project resources summary 64
Project Review Board 216
Project Review Board role 58
Project Sponsor 216
Project Sponsor role 58
Project stages 48, 110
Project status report 64
Project Status Reporting 63
Project status review 62
Project status summary 66
Project summary 63
Project time apportionment 99
Project timescale weightings 100
Project Timescales 100
Promoting good practice 97
Property addresses standards 104
Property external condition 187
Property general details 186
Property internal condition 188
Property mains supplies 187
Property Management 186
Property rooms 187
Property summary 189
Property tool kit 186
Proposals to Customers 82
Protocol 216
Prototyping 216
PSS 216
PSTN 216
PSU 216
Public key 216
Publicity Material 35
Purchase orders 200
Purpose of the Handbook 5

Q

Quality assurance 216
Quality assurance practicalities 70
Quality Products and Services 15
Quality service delivery 14
Qwerty 216

R

RAM 216
RDBMS 216
RDF 216
Record 216
Recruitment of Staff 160
Recruitment process 160
Reference sites 123
Relational database 216
Report production 28
Requisition note 200
Resource Manager role 59
Resource planning 141
Responsibilities for service levels 39
Rights of individuals 96
RISC 216
Risk Assessment 53
Risk assessment and management 89
Risk avoidance 53
Risk management 54, 130, 216
ROM 216
Router 217
Routine tasks for staff 42
RS232 217
RSA 217

S

Scanner 217
Schedule header standards 105
Schedule of rates 200
Scoping 217
Screen standards 103
Script 217
SCSI 217
SCSI-2 217
SD-RAM 217
Security breach major risks 89
Security in Systems 92
Security requirements specification 90
Security Standards 89
Security training 90
Sensitive data 96
Server 217
Service delivery perception 40
Service level agreement contents 39
Service level agreement monitor 40
Service Level Agreements 39
Shortlisting applicants 162
Sign-on standards 103
SIMM 217
Sizing rules-of-thumb 86
Skeleton programs 108
SLA 217
SMART 217
Smart card 217
Smartsuite 217
SMOG 217
Social guidelines 178
Socialising 177

INDEX

Socialising benefits 177
Software 217
Source language 217
Spam 217
Spooling 217
Spreadsheet 217
SQL 217
SSADM 217
Staff Appraisals 154
Staff charging rates 83
Staff Development 152
Staff development 152
STAFF MANAGEMENT 137
Staff report contents 141
Staff Training 153
Staffing estimates/recharges 83
Stakeholder identification 72
Stakeholder interviews 72
Standard costing 200
Standard transactions 108
Standard Transactions and Programs 108
Standards and Guidelines 20
Standards areas 20
STP 217
Strategic Activities 10
Stress causes 148
Stress Management 147
Stress management in staff 148
Stress management of oneself 149
Stress symptoms 147
Structured cabling 218
Structured programming 218
Successful projects 47
Supplier details 120
Suppliers and their products 136
Support and maintenance profit monitor 69
SVGA 218
SWIFT 218
Switch 218
SWOT 218
Sybase 218
Synchronous 218
System 218
System Design 101
System design aims 101
System design stages 101
System identification 80
System life cycle 71
System parameters standards 104
System performance 121
System performance appraisal 74
System proposal contents 82
System review 75
System Specification 98, 218
SYSTEM SPECIFICATION AND PRODUCTION 98
System Specification contents 98
System support 119
System X 218
Systems analysis 218
Systems engineering 218
Systems software 218
Systems trials 218

T

Table 218
Table standards 104
Talk21 218
Tangible benefits 77
Target hours 200
TCP/IP 218
Team Leadership 143
Team Management 141
Technical references 131
Technical requirements 81
Technical staff availability 121
Telecommunications 97
Telephone and Email Skills 25
Telephone costs 86
Telephone skills 25
Teleworking 218
TelNet 218
Tender evaluation 135
Tender invitation details 134
Tender process organisation 133
Tender Questionnaires 131
Tender selection process 135
Tendering 133
Tendering procedures 135
Tendering timetable 133
Terminal 218
Testing security 90
Thermal printer 218
Thin client 218
TickIT 218
Time analysis 180
Time management 175
Token Ring 218
Toolbar 218
TP 218
TQM 218
Trackball 218
Trading account 201
Training and development 159
Training Customers 26
Training documentation 153
Training plan production 153
Training potential areas 153
Training users 112
Trial balance 201
TTY 219

U

Underachievement management 156
Unix 219
Unix costs 86
UOM 219
UPS 219
Upwards Appraisal 159
URL 219
USB 219
User acceptance trials 219
User friendliness 122

229

User Group 219
User groups 123
User guide 219
User Guide and Training 112
User guide contents 112
User identity and password security 93
User profile record 103
UTP5 219

V

V90 219
VAR 219
VBA 219
VBS 219
VDU 219
VGA 219
Video conferencing 219
Viring 201
Virus 219
Visual Basic 219
Voicemail 219
VRAM 219

W

W3C 219
Walkthrough 219
WAN 219
WAP 219
Web 220
Web page 220
Web site 220
Webcam 220
Weekly tasks for staff 43
Windows 220
Windows 2000 220
Windows 95 220
Windows 98 220
Windows NT 220
WinZip 220
Word 220
Word processor 220
Work agreement 220
Work analysis 142
Work centre 201
Work checklist 116
Work flow 114
Work log contents 115
Work Management 114
Work request contents 115
Work scheduling and monitoring 141
Work specification and agreement 116
Working for others 174
Working hours management 175
Working your notice 169
Workstation 220
Workstation costs 85
World Wide Web 220
WORM 220

Worm 220
WP 220
Written Communications 2
WYSIWYG 220

X

X WINDOWS 220
X/OPEN 220
X25 220
X400 220
XHTML 220
XML 220

Y

Y2K 220
Yahoo 220

Z

ZIP 220
ZIP drive 220